The Book of Job

The Book of Job

*God's Answer to the Problem
of Undeserved Suffering*

Gleason L. Archer

Baker Book House
Grand Rapids, Michigan 49506

Copyright 1982 by
Gleason L. Archer

ISBN: 0–8010–0190–0

First printing, December 1982
Second printing, July 1983

Printed in the United States of America

To the memory
of my dear friend
and faithful pastor
Richard A. Swanson

Contents

Preface   7

Foreword   9

Introduction   11

Outline of the Book of Job   23

The Prologue in Heaven: Satan's Challenge
and God's Reply (1–2)   27

Job's Debate with the Three Counselors:
The First Cycle (3–14)   41

The Debate Continued: The Second Cycle (15–21)   67

The Debate Concluded: The Third Cycle (22–31)   78

The Speeches of Elihu (32–37)   90

Jehovah's Addresses to Job (38–41)   102

The Epilogue: Job's Repentance and Vindication (42)   109

Concluding Remarks   116

Bibliography   125

Preface

The incentive for this renewed study of the Book of Job came from an actual situation. It was in May 1976 that my pastor, Richard Swanson, along with his dear wife, Janis, came calling to share with me the disquieting news that they had just received about his health. His physician had diagnosed that he was suffering from lymphoma. At the age of forty-two Pastor Swanson was facing the prospect of being cut off from a very promising and successful career as leader of our local church on the North Shore of Chicago. We three discussed the crisis very earnestly, and then knelt in prayer to commit the whole matter to God. We prayed in full confidence that the Lord was abundantly able to arrest the malignancy and save him from death, no matter what the medical experts might say. But we were also aware that God might see fit to transfer him to a new assignment in glory, even though his work on earth might seem from our human viewpoint to be incomplete. It was with an added dimension of surrender that Dick presented his body once again to the Lord as a "living sacrifice," in the spirit of Romans 12:1–2.

It so happened that I was assigned the responsibility of leading the midweek prayer service at our church during June and July. Almost instinctively I turned to the Book of Job as the appropriate source for a series of Bible studies during that soul-trying period. God's Word always has an answer for every need that may arise in the life of the believer, and our need as a congregation at that juncture was to prepare ourselves for the possibility that God in His perfect will and inscrutable wisdom might take our pastor from us. Despite the immense volume of prayer and agonizing supplication that this threat evoked throughout the Free Church community on the North Shore, it was just possible that our leader would join the church triumphant before the year was out. And we who loved him so deeply and looked to him so constantly for leadership and counsel would have to face a future without him—just at a time when we needed him the most in the expanding outreach of our church.

This challenge to faith, this discipline of sorrow, served to attune us as a fellowship of believers to hear the message and teaching of Job. Out of this study came "strength for the day and bright hope for tomorrow." The strong reassurance of the perfection of God's will (contrary though it might be to our own) availed to keep us steady and knit together in loving zeal all through the succeeding months of alternate discouragement and hope that marked the progress of that dread disease, until the final phase in December, when Richard Swanson quietly slipped away into the presence of the King. And it kept us united in purpose and courage as we coped with the disappointment and the sorrow of our loss, and waited upon the Lord for the new undershepherd He had in mind for us. Ours has always been a loving, caring congregation, but during those weeks of emotional adjustment we all felt even closer to each other and more firmly committed than ever before to loyal support and promotion of the work that had meant so much to our beloved leader.

It is the earnest prayer of this writer that all who read this book and study the teaching of Job with openness of heart may find themselves leaning more confidently than ever upon the sustaining grace of God, who never makes a mistake, and who "works all things together for good to those who love Him."

Foreword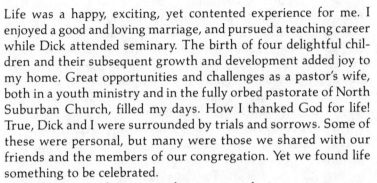

Life was a happy, exciting, yet contented experience for me. I enjoyed a good and loving marriage, and pursued a teaching career while Dick attended seminary. The birth of four delightful children and their subsequent growth and development added joy to my home. Great opportunities and challenges as a pastor's wife, both in a youth ministry and in the fully orbed pastorate of North Suburban Church, filled my days. How I thanked God for life! True, Dick and I were surrounded by trials and sorrows. Some of these were personal, but many were those we shared with our friends and the members of our congregation. Yet we found life something to be celebrated.

At the times when we are least prepared, circumstances may swiftly change. Unexpected events cause us to know for sure that we are simply clay pots and not marvelously, untouchably perfect in body. Such an event confronted our family when we experienced a dramatic, life-changing fact—our dearest earthly treasure, our husband and father, became ill and was shortly thereafter diagnosed as having a most dreadful form of lymphoma, a fast-growing, virulent, cell-type cancer. From May 1976 to Dick's death in December, we walked a difficult road. After the initial diagnosis, we desired an additional opinion. Letters came, suggesting a variety of treatments and solutions to our situation. We traveled to the Radiation Therapy Clinic at Stanford University, where we were given a more definitive diagnosis and a prescribed plan of treatment. Then came the challenge to carry on his ministry and my work while maintaining a good family atmosphere during the days and months of hard treatment: radiation followed by strong chemotherapy. Shortly after we learned of the cancer, I had covenanted with my God to continue to celebrate life as long as Dick lived. There were periods of time when it was obvious that the Holy Spirit ministered to us. On other occasions we were barely able to recognize His work until we looked back. He supplied "grace upon grace" as we chose to stand firm in that trust and faith, which early in our life together was a conscious and deliberate decision.

During these times when, for me, the circumstances were overwhelming, when I felt as if I were emotionally drowning, God's choice people came to stand by my side and to encourage me with a vision greater than mine. One such person was Gleason Archer, who had earlier experienced a similar grief. His faith, his knowledge of God's Word, and his capacity to share my experience deeply made his gracious friendship and spiritual counsel very supportive. His comfort was filled with the God he trusted.

Three basic truths continue to form the foundation for my Christian life, and these seem to have been true for Job as well. First, the Lord God was, and is, worthy of my praise and worship and love. Second, His love for me, yes, His Calvary love, remains consistent, no matter what circumstances arise. Third, this God never leaves me on my own, but through His Spirit, His Word, His servants, and my family, empowers my life.

I am thankful for this book with its honest and clear presentation regarding the suffering of God's children. It is my prayer that God will use this book in individual lives to accomplish His purposes.

Janis L. Swanson

Introduction

The Special Purpose of This Study

As I have indicated in the preface, the object of this survey of
the teaching of the Book of Job is to apply its truth and life-
strengthening power to the mind and heart of the believer. For
this reason all discussion of competing or contrary views will be
kept at a minimum, except insofar as they may help the reader to
appreciate more fully the distinctive message of this remarkable
work. In the preparation of a scholarly commentary one should,
of course, give careful attention to the varying interpretations of
Old Testament scholars who occupy a different set of presupposi-
tions from those of this author, with a view to coming to terms
with their arguments and conclusions. But the purpose of this
study manual is to allow the text of Job, inspired of God as it truly
is, to instruct us, to rebuke and correct us, and to equip us to
grapple with the hardships of life and the experiences of bereavement and loss and resultant grief, at a level that a merely critical
analysis could never hope to achieve. In other words, my concern
will be particularly with what the ancient text has to tell us, on
the assumption that its teaching message is truly and fully the
inspired, authoritative, and completely trustworthy word of God
Himself—the God and Father of our Lord Jesus Christ, the Father
of mercies and the God of all comfort. My presupposition in
dealing with this book is that it is what it purports to be—an
accurate and authentic record of an experience that actually befell
a godly believer in ancient times, a believer who was badly advised
by three would-be comforters who were ill equipped to counsel,

better advised (for the most part) by a younger man who had a
better grasp of spiritual realities than they, and then finally
admonished, humbled, and corrected by the direct teaching of the
Lord Yahweh Himself. This study assumes the reality and sinister
influence of a personal devil (who is clearly set forth as such in
this book, in harmony with the teaching of the rest of Scripture),
a supernatural being whose purpose to ensnare and destroy us is
just as real even today as is the loving desire of our Lord and
Savior Jesus Christ to redeem and transform us, and to make us
ready for eternal life in His fellowship and service, both in this
present age and in that which is to come. Readers who operate
upon any other presupposition will not be pleased or satisfied by
this presentation. Indeed they may be somewhat disturbed and
upset by it—and not solely because of its meager documentation.
It is always a bit uncomfortable to be confronted directly with the
revealed will of God in a book that one has assumed to be simply
another human search for metaphysical truth, on a par with the
scriptures and philosophical discourses of other traditions. It is
just as disturbing as to find out that the ancient, historical human
figure of Jesus of Nazareth turns out to be also the eternal, ever-
living, supremely sovereign God, who became incarnate in the
womb of the Virgin Mary. But the thinker who has become convinced by the overwhelming evidence that Jesus Christ has come
to fulfil the redemptive program of God and to speak with
absolute authority to the need of fallen man will find it logically
inevitable to accept, heed, and obey His written word as well. As
Luther wisely observed, "When the Bible speaks, God speaks."
And speak He does, in a very profound and strengthening way,
through the forty-two chapters of this marvelous book.

The Time and Place
of the Composition of Job

Unlike the other four poetic books in the Old Testament, the
Book of Job gives us no definite clue as to its author. Job himself

may have composed it after his ordeal was over, and he may have written out the substance of the dialogues while they were still fresh in his mind. The information contained in the first two chapters, relating to the encounter between God and Satan in the celestial audience chamber (1:6–12; 2:1–6) could only have been disclosed to Job by divine revelation. Yet since Job was directly addressed by God in chapters 38–42, it is not difficult to suppose that the Lord later disclosed the supernatural contest that led to his heartbreaking trials.

The narrative of Job reads like the report of a careful observer, and it could be perhaps inferred that the composer of the text itself may have been Elihu, or even some other listener to the debate whose name does not occur in the record. The third-person description of Job's virtues, attainments, and possessions in chapter 1 and also in chapter 42 certainly sounds like the work of a listener who carefully recorded the remarks of all the disputants in the case, and then later in conversation with Job himself may have learned from him the material in the prologue and epilogue, which could only have come through God's revelation to Job. If so, whoever composed this masterpiece must have been working quite closely with Job himself from start to finish. The poetic diction with which the discussions are carried on might suggest an artistic recasting of the actual words employed by the various collocutors, and yet the deviation from the very words spoken may not have been as great as we Westerners might suppose. Ancient literature from the Near East shows that not only the well-educated upper classes but also on occasion even speakers of more humble social standing were capable of expressing themselves in beautifully poetic fashion. Somewhat before the time of Job, for example, the Middle Kingdom Egyptian "Tale of the Eloquent Peasant" presents a farmer from Wadi Natrun as declaiming with great eloquence against a certain unprincipled nobleman named Djehuti-nakht on account of his injustice toward the farmer in depriving him of his donkey and all the wares he had been conveying to market. So impressive was his earnest protest, all couched in poetic style, that the governor encouraged his agents to keep the peasant protesting for several more days than needful, in order that they might write down his remarks for the governor to read. Not until then was his appeal granted and the greedy nobleman stripped of his plunder. (Compare J. B. Pritchard, *Ancient Near Eastern Texts,* third edition [Princeton: Princeton University Press, 1969], pp. 407–410. Hereafter cited as *ANET.*) The point of this reference is to show that in that culture even such prosaic transactions as arguing a legal case could be carried on in free verse. (Interestingly enough, this same Egyptian production closely resembles Job in that it opens with a prose introduction and closes with a prose epilogue, while most of the dialogue in the body of the text consists of high-flown poetry markedly resembling that of the five human collocutors of Job. This single example is enough to expose the fallacy of liberal critical theories that the poetic core of Job dates from an earlier time of composition than the prose prologue and epilogue.) A somewhat similar combination of prose and poetry is found in the "Words of Ahikar," preserved in an Aramaic version among the Elephatine Papyri of the fifth century B.C. (*ANET,* pp. 427–430).

So far as the place of composition is concerned, it is a fair inference from the close relationship between Job himself and the writing of this account that the place of origin was in the vicinity of Uz, his hometown. The location of Uz, however, is by no means certain. Outside of the Book of Job, Uz is mentioned only in Jeremiah 25:20 and Lamentations 4:21; in the former passage the kings of Uz are mentioned between Egypt and the Philistines, as objects of God's punitive wrath. In the latter, the "daughter of Edom" is said to be residing "in the land of Uz," perhaps as a result of Nebuchadnezzar's invasion of Palestine-Syria in 588–586 B.C. Uz must have been fairly close and accessible, therefore, to the refugees from Edom. The linguistic affinities indicated by the Hebrew text suggest that it was translated from a dialect of North Arabic that had absorbed many Aramaic terms. A convenient discussion of the Aramaic terms and expressions found in Job is available in Norman H. Snaith's discussion in *The Book of Job* (London: SCM, 1968), pages 104–112. But it is the contention of

A. Guillaume ("The Unity of the Book of Job," *The Annual of Leeds University, Oriental Section* 14 [1962–63], pp. 26–27) that in actuality many of the alleged Aramaisms in Job might better be classified as Arabisms. He thus deals with twenty-five of them, showing an Arabic cognate in each case. At any rate, whoever the Hebrew translator may have been (and some scholars have suggested that it might have been Moses), he seems to have been dealing with an original that was a mixture of those two tongues. It is also instructive to note that the powerful North Arabian tribe known as the Nabateans, which dominated most of Transjordan from Eilat to Damascus, has left behind a fairly extensive collection of inscriptions, largely composed in Aramaic, on stone. North Arabia, then, near the borders of Edom, furnishes the most likely locality for Uz. Certain it is that Eliphaz, the oldest of the three friends, came from Teman, a prominent center in Edom. Elihu came from the Buzites, a nation near the ancestral home of the Chaldeans in northeast Arabia.

As for the time of composition, there is no clear reference to any known historical event. The symbolic interpretation followed by most liberal critics proposes that Job is not a real historical character so much as a personification of Israel or Judah, passing through the agonizing trial of the Babylonian devastation and seventy years of captivity. But such efforts to place the composition of Job in the sixth century B.C. or later overlook the most remarkable feature to be found in the entire book. That feature is the complete absence of any reference to Moses or the twelve tribes or the Pentateuchal legislation. The only passage that has been argued as showing an awareness of the Mosaic law is Job 24:2–11, where mention is made of the wickedness of keeping pawned clothes overnight (forbidden in Exod. 22:26), the charitable measure of reserving the gleaning of the fields of the rich for the benefit of the poor (Lev. 19:9), and the monstrous evil of moving a boundary marker (Deut. 19:14). However, this passage alludes to no legal provisions at all, but simply describes the lamentable state of those who are so poor that they have to glean the fields of the rich and pawn their clothing to buy food (with

the result that they must shiver through the night). As for the
sanction against the shifting of boundary markers, this is a com-
monplace in the Code of Hammurabi and other Mesopotamian
law codes, and demonstrates no awareness at all of the juris-
prudence of the Torah. Job contains no allusion whatever to the
patriarchs, to Moses or Joshua, or to any of the judges or kings of
Israel. No other biblical work shows such a complete ignorance of
Israel or any aspect of her history. Only one conclusion can be
drawn from all of this, and that is that Job must have been
composed *outside* of Israelite circles altogether, and that it must
have been written before there ever was any such theocracy as
the commonwealth of Israel established in the land of Canaan. In
view of the undeviating commitment to monotheistic faith that
pervades the entire work, it is inconceivable that no recognition
of a monotheistic nation like Israel would occur in the extensive
theological discussions of the five collocutors in this book. In all of
the other poetic books of the Old Testament canon (the so-called
hokhmah literature) the Israelite monarchy is alluded to directly or
by way of implication; the same is true of all the other post-Mosaic
books. Only in Job is there a complete absence of such references.
This striking factor by itself renders all of the late-date theories
of the composition of Job completely at variance with the internal
evidence of the text itself. This total ignorance of Israel on the
part of a culture so close to the borders of Israel subsequent to
Joshua's conquest points unmistakably to the period of the Egyptian sojourn (1876–1445 B.C.) as the most likely period for the
origin of Job.

The Distinctive Purpose of Job

If the pre-Mosaic setting for this book is the only conclusion
that accounts for the complete silence of, or unawareness in
regard to, Israel, the only possible conclusion to draw is that Job is
actually the oldest book in the entire Bible. Even Genesis itself,

while it narrates an earlier period of history than Job, seems to have been written by Moses. There is such a clear connection between the covenant relationship of Abraham, Isaac, and Jacob to the God of Israel as the ideological basis for the commonwealth of Israel before the Lord at Mount Sinai that it is accurate to say that all of Exodus through Deuteronomy presupposes precisely the information contained in Genesis (e.g., Gen. 15:13–14).

If, then, Job turns out to be the earliest of the sixty-six books in the Bible, we must raise the question: Why was it that a work of non-Hebrew origin, completely unaware of the special relationship between God and the race of Abraham, should have been the first to be revealed? Perhaps we may find the answer to this question in the urgency of the main issue with which this book deals.

What is that issue? Nothing less than the chief stumbling block to all men's faith in the goodness and power of God as the ruler and judge over all the world. How can it ever be that calamity may befall the godly? How can a sincere and earnest believer who has all his life followed the Lord with true devotion and furnished an exemplary pattern of conduct be stricken with deadly illness or assassination, or suffer the loss of his loved ones, just as if he were some wicked offender who is ripe for judgment? And conversely, how can it be that heartless, self-seeking materialists, who care nothing for God and despise their fellow man, go through life untouched by such disasters? If God is all-powerful and all-just, how can He allow the innocent to suffer and the guilty (in some cases, at least) to be exempt from tragedy and loss? The all-too-frequent disparity between merit and fortune, between wickedness and prosperity, furnishes one of the most serious obstacles to faith that can beset the mind of the observer. Is God not really concerned about justice? Or is He too limited in power to maintain and enforce righteousness upon earth? What useful purpose can be achieved by the painful afflictions or heartbreaking bereavements that occasionally overtake even the godliest and most sincere?

The Book of Job was revealed for the purpose of answering this tormenting difficulty. In the profound insights and solemn truths taught in this remarkable work there are solid grounds given for the believer to trust God completely and submissively, even where he cannot perceive a clue as to the purpose of his own affliction. Through this heroic example of steadfastness in the face of overwhelming misfortune, and the deliverance he experienced from self-pity and bitterness of soul, God's servant Job furnishes to us all a powerful confirmation that "God works all things"— even the bitterest things—"together for good to those who love Him."

We should be careful also to note that even though Job was not informed by God as to the reason for his sufferings, this record shows that there were in fact high and noble purposes achieved through submitting him to all of the calamities he had to endure. He had been greatly honored by being chosen especially by God to demonstrate the meaning of full surrender. Satan had challenged the Lord to prove that Job's piety was based on something higher than self-interest. Satan's contention was that all so-called believers—even God's prime example, Job himself—love God for the sake of His material benefits rather than for His own sake. Take all these blessings away, including loved ones, wealth, and health, and any of these "believers," even the best of them, will turn against God in bitterness and curse Him to His face. In other words, all professing lovers of God are playing a false role, and are in reality trying to manipulate Him to their own advantage. It was a great honor indeed for Job to be chosen to prove that Satan was wrong on this very important point. Had Job been informed in advance that his coming ordeal was intended to serve this high and holy purpose, he would have found it much easier to bear his trials with cheerfulness and fortitude. But had he been so informed in advance, the test would have been invalidated. Why? Because it was essential for the victim of these trials to trust God and continue to submit to Him through them all, even though he lacked the slightest clue as to why a hitherto protective and loving God should appear to forsake him so completely to the malignity of Satan. He was left to battle with doubt and dismay as he tried

vainly to puzzle out why God had so completely turned against
him.

From this example we should learn that the same thing may
happen to believers today. They may be overtaken by the most
heartbreaking misfortunes without receiving the slightest inkling
as to their purpose. They are left to wonder through all of their
anguish: "Why did God allow this to happen to me? What have I
done to deserve it?" The example of Job proves that the Lord may
have some excellent reasons for this apparent abandonment, and
that we do not really need to know what those reasons are—until
He in His own time (perhaps after we leave this life) sees fit to
explain them to us.

God's Threefold Answer to the Problem of Undeserved Pain

Instead of saving a summary of God's solution for unmerited
suffering until the final portion of this analysis, it would perhaps
be more helpful to the reader initially to lay hold of the basic
theme that runs throughout these forty-two chapters, and thus
be the more alert to observe wherever any of these factors are
brought into view. The factors are three in number and may be
defined as follows.

First, God is worthy of our total love, adoration, and praise,
even apart from all of His benefits to us. In His infinite wisdom,
His perfection, and His power He deserves our utmost admiration
and worship. It is a tremendous privilege just to know Him and to
contemplate the marvels of His universe. But more than that, in
His special revelation of His love and care for us, and in the
supreme gift of His only begotten Son to be our Savior, our
eternal companion and friend, and the Lord of our life, God has
already bestowed upon us blessing beyond all measure. Whatever
temporal benefits we may enjoy—such as health and wealth and
dear ones, indispensable though they may seem to our earthly

happiness—pale into insignificance when compared with the gift
of God's dear Son, "in whom are hid all the treasures of wisdom
and knowledge. . . . And ye are complete in him, which is the head
of all principality and power" (Col. 2:3, 10, KJV). He who has the
Lord has all that he really needs (and far more than he deserves).
He who does not have the Lord, regardless of whatever else he
has, lives a life that is a meaningless tragedy. This, then, is the
first answer to the problem of undeserved suffering: God is
worthy of our love, even apart from all His blessings.

Second, God permits suffering in the life of the believer in
order to strengthen his faith and purify his soul. It is precisely
when the props are knocked from under us that we find ourselves
cast upon God. The more we are deprived of the temporal
supports for our earthly happiness, the more we are driven to the
Lord for our comfort and support. The more we walk through
the valley of darkness, the more aware we become of the reality
of His presence. "I will fear no evil: for thou art with me" (Ps.
23:4, KJV). Nothing contributes so much to our spiritual growth
as a period of tribulation and grief in which we learn to cherish
the Lord above all others and all else. Our greatest maturing
takes place in times of affliction and deep privation, because it is
at such times that we learn to appreciate more fully those
immeasurable blessings that no adversity can ever take from us:
the assurance of God's love, joy in the Holy Ghost, peace of
conscience, increase in grace, and perseverance therein to the end
(Westminster Shorter Catechism #36). As Romans 8:28 assures
us, God works all things (even bitter, heartbreaking things)
together for good to those who love Him. Or as we are promised
in Hebrews 12:11 (KJV; italics added): "Now no chastening for the
present seemeth to be joyous, but grievous: *nevertheless* afterward
it yieldeth the peaceable fruit of righteousness unto them that are
exercised thereby." This means, then, that no matter how intense
the agony or overwhelming the grief, we are being prepared for
fruitage. It was through his overwhelming disaster that Job was
brought to his highest potential for fruitbearing—especially the

fruit of endurance under discouragement and pressure, by which he honored and glorified the Lord even more than he had during his previous prosperity. Rightly the apostle James refers to him as a splendid model for us to follow: "You have heard of the endurance of Job and have seen the outcome of the Lord's dealings, that the Lord is full of compassion and is merciful" (James 5:11). In other words, it was precisely because of his completely undeserved and unparalleled suffering and his steadfastness in faith and submission to God that Job received the honor of becoming the chief figure in the earliest book of the Bible.

The third answer to the problem of undeserved suffering is to be found in the surpassing wisdom of our infinite God. His ways are often quite beyond our understanding, precisely because we view the issues of life from a limited, earthbound perspective. But God's viewpoint is from the throne room of heaven. He sees all things from the standpoint of eternity. His mind is moved by considerations too vast for our finite comprehension. Our part must be simply to trust Him even when we cannot understand what He is doing—or permitting, as it is with our small children when we take them in to receive their first antitetanus shot. They look up at us with alarm as the nurse approaches with her needle, and plead, "Don't let that lady hurt me with that sharp thing she has in her hand!" Much as we sympathize with their alarm and their pain, we know that it is the part of true love for us to allow them this temporary hurt in order to safeguard them against far greater harm in the time to come. Whenever we do not understand why our heavenly Father allows us to be afflicted, we are simply to trust Him fully, believing that He knows what is best for our benefit and for His glory. And we may be sure that the time will come in the glory of His presence when we shall understand the reason for our earthly woe. Or, as in the case of Job, we may even come to an insight as to God's wise and loving purpose in submitting us to the trials we could not understand as long as they were besetting us. And it may be that we too shall be privileged to testify, as Job doubtless did, to all of the believing community that God was faithful to us, and did all things well on our behalf.

This, then, is the third answer: that God's thoughts and ways have eternity in view, and are moved by considerations too vast and profound for our finite comprehension.

Outline of the Book of Job

I. **The Prologue in Heaven: Satan's Challenge and God's Reply (1-2)**

   A. From Prosperity to Woe and Tragic Loss (1)

   B. Rejected by Society and His Own Wife, and Marred by Hideous Illness, Job Is Visited by Three Old Friends (2)

II. **Job's Debate with the Three Counselors: The First Cycle (3-14)**

   A. Job Expresses His Despair (3)

   B. Eliphaz Kindly Protests and Urges Humble Submission (4)

   C. Eliphaz Exhorts Job to Repentance (5)

   D. Job's Remonstrance and Defense Against Eliphaz (6-7)

   E. Bildad's Rejoinder to Job: Your Sniveling Complaints Impugn the Justice of God and Attack the Foundation of the Moral Order! (8)

   F. Job's Response to Bildad: No Mortal Man May Argue His Innocence Before the Almighty; Yet He May Protest Against Cruelly Unfair Treatment (9-10)

   G. Zophar's Response to Job: God Is Right and You Are Wrong! Better Get Right with Him, For the Wicked Are Without Hope (11)

   H. Job Answers His Accusers (12-14)

III. **The Debate Continued: The Second Cycle (15-21)**

   A. Eliphaz Accuses Job of Presumption in Disregarding the Wisdom of the Ancients and Criticizing God As Unjust (15)

B. Job's Replay to Eliphaz: It Is Easy to Berate a Victim of Misfortune; Nevertheless I Will Appeal to God from My Unjust Accusers, For He Is My Last Resort (16–17)

C. Bildad's Reply to Job's Rejection: This Man Is Simply Receiving His Just Deserts (18)

D. Job Responds to Bildad's Tirade with a Strong Appeal to God (19)

E. Zophar Replies That Job Has Rejected God Himself by Criticizing His Administration of Justice (20)

F. Job Counters with a Challenge to Zophar That He Is Out of Touch with Reality; Not All Injustices Are Righted in This Life (21)

IV. **The Debate Concluded: The Third Cycle (22–31)**

A. Eliphaz Denounces Job's Criticism of God's Justice (22)

B. Job Responds to Eliphaz That God Knows He Is Without Guilt, and Yet in His Providence He Permits Temporary Success for the Wicked (23–24)

C. Bildad Scoffs at Job's Direct Appeal to God (25)

D. Job's Rejoinder to Bildad: God Is Indeed Perfectly Wise and Absolutely Sovereign in Punishment of the Wicked, But Not in the Stereotyped, Simplistic Way Described by My Critics (26–27)

E. The Search for Transient Treasures Contrasted with the Discovery of True Wisdom, Which Transcends All Other Treasures (28)

F. Job's Concluding Complaint and Solemn Disclaimer of Iniquity (29–31)

V. **The Speeches of Elihu (32–37)**

A. Elihu Enters into the Debate to Break the Impasse (32)

B. Elihu Charges Job with Presumption in Criticizing God, Not Recognizing That God May Have a Loving Purpose Even in Allowing Job to Suffer (33)

C. Elihu Declares That Job Has Impugned God's Integrity in Upholding the Moral Law, and Has Claimed That It Does Not Pay to Lead a Godly Life in This Ungodly World (34)

    D. Elihu Urges Job to Wait Patiently for the Lord to Act Whenever and However He Sees Fit (35)

    E. Notwithstanding Job's Criticisms, The Lord Almighty Still Remains the Avenger of Injured Justice, Even Though He May Administer His Providence in Ways Beyond Our Comprehension (36)

    F. Elihu Continues to Argue, from Man's Inability to Understand Fully God's Workings in Nature, That Human Observers Can Hardly Expect to Understand Adequately His Dealings in Administering Justice and Mercy (37)

VI. Jehovah's Addresses to Job (38–41)

    A. No Man Is Competent to Pass Judgment upon the Dealings of the Almighty (38:1–38)

    B. God Probes Job's Knowledge of Controlling and Feeding Wild Animals and Birds (38:39—39:30)

    C. The God Who Made the Behemoth and the Leviathan Is Far Beyond the Competence of Man to Criticize or Correct (40–41)

VII. The Epilogue: Job's Repentance and Vindication (42)

    A. Job Passes Contrite and Unsparing Judgment upon Himself (42:1–6)

    B. God's Condemnation of Eliphaz, Bildad, and Zophar (42:7–9)

    C. Job's Restoration to the Favor of His Community and Relatives (42:10–11)

    D. Job's Renewed Prosperity and Lengthened Span of Life (42:12–17)

VIII. Concluding Remarks

I. The Prologue in Heaven:
Satan's Challenge and God's Reply (1-2)

A. From Prosperity to Woe and Tragic Loss (1)

1. (1:1-3) Job's character was sterling and his wealth unrivaled.

a. (:1) Job was completely committed to God and His holy standards of conduct and life: "blameless" (*tām*) implies complete sincerity and integrity of character; "upright" (*yāshār*) implies complete fairness and honesty; "fearing God" (*yᵉrē' 'elōhīm*) indicates that he feared and abhorred above all else the violation of the known will of God in any particular, because of his utter devotion to God in his life; "turning away from evil" (*sār mērā'*) implies that no form of wickedness or vice had any attraction for him, but he consistently shunned and avoided and withdrew himself from everything unworthy in the sight of God. This first verse makes it very clear to us that Job was a completely sincere and godly man, with no secret sins to cover up. Furthermore, he was a force for righteousness in his community.

It is a striking feature of this book (as already pointed out in the introduction) that Job lived in a consistently monotheistic culture. Polytheism is by no means unknown to these people, for at one point Job solemnly disavows any involvement in the worship of the sun and moon (31:26-27) even though these deities were highly regarded by the South Arabians, according to many of their inscriptions that date from the first millennium B.C. and honor the moon god as 'Ilumquh and Sami' and the sun goddess as *Dhāt-Ḥimyān* (cf. *ANET,* p. 663). But none of the disputants personally recognizes any other gods besides Yahweh or, as they usually refer to Him, *'Elōah* or *Shaddai* (which occurs thirty-one times in Job). He is for them the creator of all things that are, the omnipotent sovereign over the entire universe, a personal God who is interested in each one of his creatures, and who is deeply concerned to maintain the standards of holiness as the sustainer of the moral law. It is, of course, this pure and uncompromising monotheism that inclines evolution-minded critics to argue for a sixth-century date for the composition of Job, since the forthright proclamation of monotheism they tend to date no earlier than Amos in 760–755 B.C. But this line of reasoning views the development of religious thought as a gradual process based upon mere human initiative, rather than a special revelation by God to man, as the Bible itself constantly affirms. If a personal God was known to Adam, our first forefather, and if He manifested Himself to Noah as his deliverer from the flood, it is difficult to see why the monotheism of Job and all his companions points to the first millennium any more than it does to 1800 B.C., when the knowledge of the one true God, handed down to their forefathers by Shem, the son of Noah, might still have been faithfully maintained in various pockets of true religion among the Semites of the Near East. (Balaam the son of Beor, a fifteenth-century prophet of Yahweh, figures prominently in Numbers 22–24, even though he too came from a non-Israelite background. The same is true of Moses' Midianite father-in-law, Jethro, and also of Caleb the son of Jephunneh, who was a Kenizzite [Num. 32:12].) It is a mistake to suppose that the knowledge of the one true God was restricted to Abraham and his descendants, even though idolatry may have taken over most of the Middle East by that time. (For further discussion of early Semitic and Sumerian monotheism, see this author's *Survey of Old Testament Introduction* [Chicago: Moody, 1973], pp. 142–145. Hereafter cited as *SOTI.*)

b. (:2, 4–5) Job's material prosperity was found first of all in the ten children who were born to him, and who apparently had become young adults by the time of Job's calamity. They each had homes of their own and spent their time fellowshiping with one another. With no less than seven sons to carry on the family line, Job's position in society seemed very secure indeed, and the perpetuation of his name and reputation beyond his lifetime seemed to be a foregone conclusion.

Yet whether Job's children had embraced their father's faith and godly lifestyle was more than doubtful. Little is recorded along this line, but we may gather from their father's concern about their moral life and their reverence (or irreverence) toward God that their relationship with God was rather perfunctory and that Job had reason to feel uneasy about their souls. At any rate he continued to follow them with his love and faithful intercession before the Lord with sacrifice and prayer. And when they were all wiped out in a single disaster, this must have contributed much to his agonizing regret and grief, for he could not be sure that any of them had died in a state of salvation. Apparently this was too tender a subject for him even to speak of in his conversations with his three visitors.

c. (:3) Job was reputed to be the richest man of his time in all the region of Qedem (for the word translated as "east" may refer to the geographical region of Edom and the Transjordan known in the Assyrian records as Qadmu). Certainly it appears in the "Tale of Sinuhe" (1.29) as a definite geographical district in which Sinuhe stayed for a year and a half (*ANET,* p. 19). In that economy Job's wealth consisted largely of enormous herds of livestock: 7,000 sheep, 3,000 camels, 500 yoke of oxen, and 500 donkeys, to say nothing of his many servants. He was the largest stockholder on Wall Street, so to speak. Thus it could be said that this godly man had proved to be a good businessman, a fine citizen, and a father of a large family. As such, he enjoyed the highest standing of any man in his community, and was greatly esteemed and sought after by all who knew him. A truly enviable combination of blessings—and yet before long they were all to be stripped away from him. He was presently to learn by personal experience that, as Jesus said, "A man's life consisteth not in the abundance of the things which he possesseth" (Luke 12:15, KJV).

2. (1:6–12) God permits Satan to test Job's faith.

a. (:6) This scene of God sitting in counsel with His holy angels occurs several times in Scripture (I Kings 22:19; Isa. 6:1–3; Dan. 7:9–10; Rev. 5:6–14). Often these angels are referred to as "sons of God" (*beney 'elōhīm*), for angels too were begotten by God, just as truly as were humans (who are also referred to as *beney 'elōhīm* in Gen. 6:2; Deut. 14:1; 32:5; Hos. 1:10). Although angels are without physical bodies, they yet possess many supernatural powers.

But into this holy assembly slips a sly intruder who was once himself a citizen of heaven. This was Satan (meaning "Adversary"), intent as usual upon discrediting the Lord and hindering His program of redemption. But the question arises at this point: How did Satan get admitted to this heavenly council? This would seem to be a most surprising development indeed. In Revelation 21:27 we are told that nothing abominable or profane will gain admittance to the city of God, and we may safely assume that this has always been the case in God's heavenly throne room. But there are at least two lower levels of "heaven" (cf. II Cor. 12:2), and it is possible that this council session was held at a level closer to earth—perhaps even close enough to Satan's area of activity, which fits him for the title "the prince of the power of the air" (Eph. 2:2). The devil seems to be permitted entrance in cases where, prior to the cross, man's disobedience toward God and His law gives him an opening to invade the sinner's heart, lure him into grosser sin, and then at the last to appear as a witness against him before God's judgment throne. So it was in Zechariah 3:1, where Satan accused Joshua, the high priest of Israel, before the angel of the Lord, seeking to have him and his errant nation condemned for their transgressions, in strict accordance with the law. The devil is always eager to support and further all retributive justice that is meted out to those whom he has duped or abetted in their wickedness. He has always been an enemy of forgiveness and grace, since they rob him of those who would otherwise be permanent denizens of hell, firmly under his control.

One other unexpected feature of this confrontation is found in the casual, relaxed manner in which God speaks to Satan. A far sterner and harsher tone would seem appropriate in such a situation. But there are two special factors at work here that should not be overlooked. The first is that as the almighty and all-knowing sovereign of the universe, God has no ground for uneasiness or alarm at Satan's presence, for in God's eyes he is a defeated foe, a clever but ineffectual opponent who is destined for complete overthrow and eternal confinement in the lake of fire and brimstone appointed for him in Revelation 20:10. The second factor is that Satan's cynical challenge as to the possibility of genuine love and faith needed to be answered once and for all. His skeptical depreciation of all professed piety as merely a cloak for self-interest raised an issue that was of utmost importance for the entire human race. It could be dealt with only by an extreme test such as was in store for Job, God's prime example of sincere commitment. From this standpoint it was extremely important for the devil to raise his protest, that in actuality God was self-deceived if He even imagined that any Adamite could ever rise beyond the level of self-interest to a genuine self-surrender to the will and glory of God entirely for His own sake. For Satan was well aware that if the believer's ultimate motive for becoming "converted" is to escape hell and get to heaven, this is simply enlightened self-interest, and he therefore still belongs to the realm of darkness. It still means a rejection of the first and great commandment: "Thou shalt love the LORD thy God with all thy heart, and with all thy soul, and with all thy might" (Deut. 6:5, KJV).

b. (:7) God inquires of Satan, "Where do you come from?" Of course He already knew the answer, for "all things are open and laid bare to the eyes of Him with whom we have to do" (Heb.

4:13). But this query furnished a convenient opening for the conversation (somewhat similar to God's "Where art thou?" addressed to Adam right after the fall). Satan's vague answer, that he had just taken an observational world tour, furnished an excellent platform for the Lord's second question.

c. (:8) The second question implied a challenge to Satan: "Have you in your world tours ever noticed My true servant, Job?" Here was a splendid example of one on whom Satan had no hold, for he was "a blameless and upright man, fearing God and turning away from evil" (exactly the same Hebrew terms used here as in verse 1). This example of a genuine, godly believer served to goad Satan into exasperation; Job was one who had gotten away! This came as a dishonor to the cause of hell; Satan's record as a mancatcher was seriously tarnished!

d. (:9–11) Satan replied according to his own sincere conviction: that like every other religious person, Job was basically a phony. All of the protection and prosperity God had granted him all his life had simply bolstered his pride and contributed to his self-interest. Who wouldn't be glad to serve the Lord as Job had, if he too could have all the work of his hands so blessed, and his possessions so increased? There may even be a note of frustration in Satan's comment, for that protective "hedge . . . on every side" had apparently thwarted all malign schemes to cause him hardship and loss. Job was no better than a protected hothouse flower.

In order to prove his cynical analysis of Job's heart, the devil challenged God to take all of Job's temporal blessings away from him. Then God would soon find out the hypocritical basis of Job's piety. He guaranteed that this vaunted example of faith would turn against the Lord like every other disappointed self-seeker in the human race, and would bitterly curse God to His face. Then Satan could remain personally reassured that God's requirement laid upon both angels and men, that they should love their creator with all their heart, would once again be demonstrated as utterly impossible to fulfill. In this way Satan would feel the more vindicated for his own primeval revolt against God (Isa. 14:12–15; Rev. 12:7–9).

e. (:12) God accepted Satan's challenge. If Job's love was basically a matter of self-seeking, a mere profession of unconditional love for God entirely for His own sake, then the sooner that was known, the better. And so God was willing to incur all of the risk of misrepresenting His own love and faithfulness through permitting such an overwhelming combination of misfortunes. This was the only way in which the factor of hidden self-interest could be ferreted out. As already indicated, it was this entire lack of explanation to Job that was vital for the validity of the test itself. No inkling of the heavenly wager should be imparted to the victim himself while he was going through the experience, lest he artificially firm up his courage as a candidate for a hero's crown in such a cosmic contest.

3. (1:13–19) Satan inflicts Job with four crushing disasters.

a. (:13–15) The cruelty of Satan's timing was heightened by the almost simultaneous nature of all four calamities, and that too on a day of celebration on the part of Job's ten children (v. 13). The oxen and donkeys were captured as booty by a band of Sabean raiders, who killed all of Job's farmhands as they tried to resist. The Sabeans came from what is now Yemen and South Yemen, on the southwestern coast of Arabia. At this earlier period, perhaps 900 years before that friendlier queen of Sheba who came to see Solomon in Jerusalem, these southern tribesmen made part of their living by piracy and rapine.

b. (:16) The 7,000 sheep, which formed such an important element of Job's holdings, were destroyed in a most astonishing way—by what we would call today "an act of God," but which in this instance was really an act of Satan, permitted by God. This must have been the most terrible electrical storm that ever occurred. Possibly the flare-up of a wilderness brush fire that completely encircled its victims added to the dreadful loss of life.

c. (:17) The raiders who took the camels came from Chaldean Arabia, probably in the northeastern coast near modern Kuwait and the oil sheikhdoms just to the south of it. These fierce marauders were equally aggressive by land and by sea. Much later, in the early seventh century B.C., their penetration up the Euphrates by their swift warships finally made them masters of Babylon itself. They founded a dynasty of which Nebuchadnezzar became the most outstanding representative. But even in the time of Abraham they seem to have controlled a portion of Sumeria near the shore of the Persian Gulf, thus furnishing the basis for calling Abraham's native city "Ur of the Chaldeans." (This, of course, served to distinguish it from the more northerly city of Ur that was located somewhat nearer to Haran and to Ebla, whose newly discovered commercial accounts make mention of it. But by no stretch of the imagination could *this* Ur be connected with the Chaldeans in the nineteenth century B.C.). That there should be more than one city by this name is not surprising, for *Urum* in Akkadian meant "the city," and was probably cognate with the Hebrew word *'îyr,* the usual term for a fortified city or town.

It should be noted that the capture of 3,000 fleet-footed camels called for a good deal of careful strategy. The experienced Chaldean raiders therefore organized themselves into three separate platoons, distributed in such a way as to cut off every possible exit. Thus they entrapped both the cameltenders and the animals themselves, and allowed only a single survivor to escape.

d. (:18–19) The cruelest blow of all was reserved by Satan for the last. This calamity would surely break Job's spirit and turn him into a bitter, cursing rebel against God. This was the catastrophic hurricane that destroyed the entire mansion in which Job's ten children were banqueting together, thus snuffing out their lives at one fell swoop. To be so suddenly bereft of such a large number of children all at once, and to be left completely childless, was a calamity almost exceeding all belief.

At this point the question arises as to whether it was right for God to allow such a frightful loss of innocent lives, simply to put one man to the test. Was this not a very great injustice to the children themselves? The answer to this difficulty can be found only in the inscrutable knowledge and wisdom of God Himself. He alone knows what is in the heart of each man, and He even foreknows all of their future responses to the proffers of divine grace that might come to them in their later life. Had they lived on for another fifty years, it is quite possible that there would have been no difference in their reaction to God's call. Those who had already given their hearts to the Lord would doubtless have remained true to the decision made as young people. And those who had resisted giving the true allegiance of their hearts to God until this time might very well have continued to do so throughout their future years. If it is possible for a single individual to make such a momentous lifetime decision in his latter teens, it is equally possible for ten. God may be trusted to do the right and fair thing in every instance, since He possesses that knowledge and that wisdom we mortals so abysmally lack.

4. (1:20-22) Job responds to his terrible losses.

a. (:20) Job's initial reaction was one of boundless grief and sorrow. Reeling under the impact of these successive strokes of financial loss, the loss of all his faithful servants (many of whom must have been dear to his heart), and above all, the loss of all his beloved children, he was led to expressions of mourning characteristic of the ancient Near East: he tore up the clothes he was wearing at the time he heard the news, and he shaved his hair from his head (in lieu of tearing it out with his hands, as the alternative custom prescribed). As the victim of such unparalleled misfortunes, he felt too crushed in heart to put up any false front of cheerful courage.

Yet Job did something more than slump down into utter despair or paroxysms of grief; he turned to the Lord God, from whom he had received all of these blessings in the first place. "He fell to the ground and worshiped."

b. (:21) Job, in his prayer to God, resigned himself humbly and submissively to His will, even though he could not understand it. Even in this emotional extremity Job remembered that he and all of his loved ones and possessions really belonged to the Lord who had given them to him. And so he openly acknowledged before the Almighty that He had a perfect right to do with His own whatever He chose to.

Job realized also that when he came into the world as a newborn baby, he possessed absolutely nothing of this world's goods. When it came his time to die, he would likewise pass away into the next life without any of his earthly possessions to accompany him. He would stand completely naked, as it were, before the Lord as he entered into His presence. As Paul remarked in I Timothy 6:7, "we brought nothing into the world, so we cannot take anything out of it either." Job had not allowed himself to become more enamored of God's gifts than of the God who had given them.

c. (:22) Thus it was that Job passed his first testing with flying colors. "Through all this Job did not sin, nor did he blame God." By this humble submission, expressing full acceptance of God's strange and unaccountable providence, he completely avoided the fierce rebelliousness that Satan had so confidently expected. On the contrary, Job succeeded in making a liar out of the prince of lies!

B. *Rejected by Society and His Own Wife,*
   and Marred by Hideous Illness,
   Job Is Visited by Three Old Friends (2)

1. (2:1-6) A second confrontation in heaven is described.

a. (:1-3) After the same opening exchange as in chapter 1, God points out to Satan that all of his cruel blows of misfortune have not availed to turn Job from his godliness and integrity (v. 3). Even under the impact of unfair and completely unwarranted affliction, he has not responded the way Satan confidently predicted that he would. "He still holds fast his integrity, although you incited Me against him, to ruin him without cause" (v. 3).

b. (:4–5) Baffled and embarrassed before God and all His heavenly court, Satan does not bother to admit that he was wrong. Instead, he grasps for some kind of vindication for his cynicism by arguing that Job still maintains his peace with God in order to protect his health—the last asset he has, yet a very valuable asset. "Yes, that is it," reasons Satan. "He's afraid to express his deep bitterness because he might be stricken by serious illness or death if he railed at God the way he really wanted to."

The devil then proposes an even more severe test: the loss of Job's health and the indignity of developing a repulsive appearance because of skin disease. "Skin for skin," he argues excitedly. "Put forth Thy hand, now, and touch his bone and his flesh; he will curse Thee to Thy face" (v. 5). Satan felt that if his hard-pressed victim could simply lose his noble appearance and bearing, he would then be banished from his home to the city dump. As long as Job retained the sympathy and comfort of his neighbors and friends, he might still muster up enough fortitude or enough courage to persevere through all of his misfortunes. But once he became a chronic invalid, with offensive breath and hideous appearance, he would surely lose heart, fall into bitterness and despair, and feel himself to be completely forsaken in the universe, abandoned by both God and man. This was surely a diabolical maneuver on Satan's part, and it had every prospect of succeeding.

c. (:6) But what Satan did not know about Job's stubborn faith was very well known to God. And so once again God gave Satan permission to do his worst against this noble, righteous saint, except for actually taking his life. If the test was to be completely and absolutely decisive, Job's faith had to be put under the utmost pressure that Satan could bring against it. "Behold, he is in your

power, only spare his life." So saying, God affirmed His sublime
confidence that His servant would not break under the merciless
assault of the forces of hell.

2. (2:7-8) Satan brings Job to the misery of the dunghill.
A single boil can be a source of great discomfort, but Job found
himself covered with them from head to foot. His loathesome
appearance only intensified the agony of his pain. In abject misery
he could only hobble out of his home, out of the gate of his city,
and make his way to the municipal dump. There he hunted for a
few broken pieces of pottery so that he could scrape away the
encrusted pus that oozed from all his angry red sores. It was a
perfect setting for a slow, degrading death to overtake him.

3. (2:9-10) Job is abandoned by his wife.

a. (:9) Deeply resentful at the loss of the family's wealth and of
all the children, Job's wife was seething with rebellion against God
for allowing such dreadful things to befall her and her fine,
upstanding husband. But she could not stand Job's continuing
calm and quietness, at a time when he should be loudly lamenting
and expressing his hatred of God for treating him so. How could
he be so lacking in spirit as to let all of this happen to him without
rebellion and protest?

b. (:10) Job's wife is rebuked for her folly, and then leaves him to
his fate. She bitterly asked, "What use is it for Job to pretend
commitment and loyalty to a God who has so betrayed him? Why
doesn't Job simply face the fact that God has unjustly abandoned
him without cause?" In her view, God was to be roundly condemned for His failure to honor the debt of gratitude He owed to
her husband for leading such a godly, virtuous life. She supposed
that the Lord God was put under obligation by any believer who
obeyed His law with faithfulness and integrity. (Such a viewpoint,
all too common among mankind in general, overlooks the fact
that in no interpersonal transactions do we consider that the

lender of money is put under obligation by his debtor when the loan is repaid!) Her only counsel to her miserable, pain-racked husband was, "Do you still hold fast your integrity (*tummāh*)" when God has so violated His own integrity toward you, and is therefore no longer worthy of your allegiance or respect? The only thing left to do is "curse God and die!" (v. 9).

Most husbands have 20/20 vision when it comes to perceiving the errors or drawbacks of their wives, and in an altercation they are apt to tell them so. But in this case Job was altogether warranted in his judgment when he rejected her blasphemous suggestion and sternly rebuked her: "You speak as one of the foolish women speaks. Shall we indeed accept good from God and not accept adversity?" In other words, a giver has a perfect right also to be a withholder, for a true gift is given not under compulsion (else it would be the mere payment of a debt) but out of grace. Therefore to discontinue the bestowal of wealth and life and bodily health must lie within the prerogative of Him who earlier bestowed those blessings.

In addition, to renounce God is as pointless as sawing off the base of the branch upon which you are perched. If there is such a reality as justice, if there is a true difference between right and wrong, it must in each case be derived from the God who created man and the entire moral order. Man can no more be more righteous than God (and therefore qualified to condemn Him as unjust) than water can rise above its source. The only possible source of moral consciousness or the binding character of the moral law is God Himself. Therefore an injustice on God's part must be only apparent, not real. Therefore also what Job's wife was saying was self-contradictory nonsense. For Job to curse God would be tantamount to cursing himself. All of his identity and the meaning of his very existence was ultimately derived from God.

This is the last we hear from Job's wife. What she did after he rebuked her we are not told. But we are certainly left to infer that that was the end of their marriage. We may suppose that among the other comforting blessings in store for Job (according to chapter 42) was a new, more compatible, and more spiritually-minded wife!

4. (2:11-13) Three friends come to visit and comfort Job.

a. (:11) The report of Job's misfortunes spread throughout the entire region of North Arabia, Edom, and Transjordan. Friends who had dealt with him and highly respected him over the years were deeply concerned, and three of them decided to pay him an extended visit and do what they could to counsel and assist him.

The first of these was Eliphaz the Temanite. Teman was a district and town named after Teman (*Tēymān,* meaning "right hand" or "south"), the grandson of Esau (Gen. 36:11). The inhabitants of Teman cultivated wisdom (*ḥokhmāh,* consisting of proverbs and philosophic reflections pertaining to relations with God and society and the rules for successful living). Eliphaz was probably the oldest of the three. He was a pious sage who endeavored to combine penetrative insight with compassion.

The second was Bildad the Shuhite. Assyrian inscriptions refer to a *Shūḥu* territory of Arameans on the west bank of the Euphrates River. This may have been the city from which Bildad (whose full name, according to W. F. Albright's suggestion, may have been Yabil-Dadum) came. Or there may have been another *Shūḥu* located in the Edomite region, of which we have no knowledge as yet. A third possibility (favored by H. F. Beck in the *Interpreter's Dictionary of the Bible* [Nashville: Abingdon, 1962], vol. 4, p. 341) is that the word *Shuhite* refers to ancestry rather than city of origin. There seems to have been an Arab tribe descended from Abraham by Keturah through their son *Shūḥah* (Gen. 38:2), and his descendants would be known as Shuhites. Yet the fact that Eliphaz and Zophar are identified by the names of their cities might raise the presumption that Bildad came from a city called *Shūḥu.* And it is by no means impossible that that city might have been the one on the Euphrates, for which there is at least some inscriptional evidence. As for Bildad himself, he was evidently a scholar steeped in traditional lore and an expert in established opinions.

The third friend, Zophar the Naamathite, probably came from Na'ameh, which has been identified with Djebel-en-Na'ameh, a mountainous area in northwestern Arabia. He may have been the youngest of the three, but at any rate he was the most impetuous of them all in debate and marked by intolerate dogmatism, with no attempt to show consideration or respect toward those who disagreed with him.

b. (:12–13) Upon their arrival at the outskirts of Uz the three saw the pitiable figure of their revered and aristocratic friend, who was reduced to such a wretched appearance and state that they could barely recognize him. Appalled that such a dreadful reversal of fortune was possible in human experience, their compassion was stirred to the utmost, and they could only sink speechless to the ground beside Job. And to their credit they did the very best thing for him that could have been done. They kept silent—and that for a whole week. They could not find words adequate for such an unrelieved tragedy, and yet that they really cared was well attested by the loyalty with which they stayed beside him. Job was no longer alone; he still had three friends who were willing to give him fellowship and sympathy in all of his woe.

II. Job's Debate with the Three Counselors: The First Cycle (3–14)

A. Job Expresses His Despair (3)

1. (3:1–10) Job curses the day he was born.

It was all very well for Job to put on a brave front of calm acceptance of the Lord's will as he argued with his wife. But now that he was encircled by old friends who had come from great distances to comfort him, Job finally felt free to express the profound grief that was building up within him. It was true enough that God had a right to remove him from all of his temporal comforts and blessings, but there comes a degree of privation and misery that robs life of its very reason for being. If this is to be the outcome of his earthly existence, then his birthday should be a black and cursed anniversary, for he really should not have been born at all. He should have died in his mother's womb.

Behind this bitter lament lurks a deep misunderstanding about the basic meaning of life. Job seemed to share, in a measure at least, in the almost universal human assumption that life without happiness is not worth living. But this assumption cannot be justified in the light of God's revelation. Concerning many of God's honored saints we read in Hebrews 11:35–38 that they were tortured, that they experienced mockings and scourgings, imprisonment and chains, and that those who were not martyred "went about in sheepskins, in goatskins, being destitute, afflicted, ill-treated" (v. 37). And yet their lives counted for God. Though they were deprived of earthly happiness, they left behind them a name of honor and a noble example for others to follow. We are grievously mistaken if we suppose that the purpose of life is happiness, or that any man has a prescriptive right to happiness. We have been created in the image of God for something far more exalted than happiness, and that is for the glory of God. How much happiness did our Savior enjoy as the forces of evil closed in upon Him prior to His crucifixion? He "endured the cross, despising the shame. . . . For consider Him who has endured such hostility by sinners against Himself. . . . You have not yet resisted to the point of shedding blood in your striving against sin" (Heb. 12:2–4). Jesus' life could hardly be described as a happy life, although He must have enjoyed happier times in His early life, prior to His three-year ministry and the sufferings of Passion Week.

And yet I should hasten to add that Jesus and the martyred saints of Bible history experienced something better than happiness; they had joy. Happiness to a certain extent depends upon external circumstances; true joy is independent of circumstances, because it derives from a right relationship with God. If we have

believed God's promise, put our trust in His mercy, and surrendered completely to His will, then none of the vicissitudes or
changing circumstances of life can rob us of that joy. Life may rob
us of happiness, but never of joy or profound inward peace.
"These things I have spoken unto you, that My joy may be in you,
and that your joy may be made full" (John 15:11). "Peace I leave
with you; My peace I give to you; not as the world gives, do I give
to you" (John 14:27).

But Job, as he considered the ruination of all his earthly hopes
and expectations and the painful disfigurement of his tortured
body, felt that continuance in life was from this point quite meaningless and therefore that it was a mistake (*God's* mistake) for him
to have been born in the first place.

2. (3:11–19) Job meditates on the better world beyond the grave.

With real longing Job looks away from his present misery to
that peaceful land on the other side of the grave, where the souls
of men—whatever their station in life might have been—enjoy
sweet rest and peace. "There the wicked cease from raging, And
there the weary are at rest. . . . And the slave is free from his
master" (vv. 17, 19). How remarkable that in this earliest written
book of the Bible there should appear such a clear and definite
hope of heaven! It is interesting to observe that Job in 3:14 may be
referring to the Pharaohs, for as the Arabic Bible renders it, he
speaks of "kings who build pyramids for themselves." Koehler-
Baumgartner's Hebrew lexicon suggests that $h^a r\bar{a}b\bar{o}t$ in this passage refers to pyramids rather than ruins; the verb for "rebuild" is
really *bānāh*, "build." (Those who construct an evolutionary pattern
for the development of Israel's religion are compelled by a passage
such as this to assign to Job a postexilic date; their preconceived
theories and question-begging assumptions force them to do so,
despite the decisive internal evidence that Job is pre-Mosaic.)

Job understands that stillborn infants would likewise be received into that land of safety and freedom from tyranny and
fear, and enjoy the sweet rest of those who have died in the faith.
"How much better this would have been for me than my survival
through infancy and maturity to arrive at such a tragic end as has

now come upon me!" In so saying, Job seems to impute to God a poor decision in his case. At the very least, Job makes it plain that if he had been given a choice, he would (in the light of what he knows now) have much preferred not to be born in the first place.

3. (3:20–26) Prolonged suffering is senseless.

What point, protests Job, is there in prolonging the days of the hapless, hopeless, suffering victims of misfortune? If they long for release through death, why should they not be permitted to die? Without enjoyment, what purpose is there in mere survival? "I can do nothing but weep and groan, and even the thought of food is loathesome to me. Everything I could have feared in the way of affliction and loss has already befallen me, and I can find nothing else worth living for." Nor can he find any relief from the pressures of restlessness and turmoil; there is never any lessening of his agony.

This entire chapter, then, is the expression of deep depression, the outburst of a soul pushed beyond all endurance. This shows us the extent to which discouragement can go, even in the life of a true believer, once he has been subjected to a prolonged period of mental anguish and physical torment. As he looked at his wretched circumstances, Job could see absolutely nothing to relieve the intense gloom of complete discouragement, caught as he was in the visegrip of total disaster. He had lost everything that makes life worth living, and all inner peace and poise had forsaken him.

B. *Eliphaz Kindly Protests*
    and Urges Humble Submission (4)

1. (4:1–6) Eliphaz reminds Job of his past role of giving comfort and encouragement to others facing hardship and sorrow. Now he should not miss the opportunity of following his own admonitions to others. "Does not that reverence for God and confidence in His goodness that you enjoined upon others avail now to lift you up from discouragement, especially in view of the integrity of your own testimony to the world in days gone by?" This exhortation to practice what Job has preached was certainly appropriate, but whether it was well timed in view of Job's emotional state after such a long ordeal and after such crushing losses remains highly questionable. At this stage a more helpful approach would be to say, "My dear friend, what a terrible ordeal you have been through! I can imagine how you feel."

2. (4:7-11) Yet Job's implied criticism of God for permitting his happiness to be shattered and his health to be broken raises a very serious theological problem. How could a holy and righteous God ever allow disaster and death to befall a person who is truly guiltless? As custodian and administrator of His own moral law, this would be utterly impossible, argues Eliphaz. We live in a world where virtue is rewarded and evil is punished: "According to what I have seen, those who plow iniquity And those who sow trouble harvest it" (v. 8). We must clearly understand that the truly innocent do not perish, nor are the truly upright ever destroyed.[1]

Note that this is the opening presentation of a theological position that is earnestly and persistently maintained by the three counselors throughout the entire debate. Three important facets are involved in this teaching.

The first is that God is indeed a faithful arbiter of the enforcement of the moral law. Job is just as firmly insistent upon this as are the three. The only question is whether His ultimate punishment of sinners and vindication of saints is completely carried out in this life.

---

1. The reference to the lions in verses 10-11 is disputed by commentators; some have even suggested that these two verses have accidentally been inserted in the wrong place. It is, however, possible to understand the fiercely roaring lion as the belligerently aggressive human rebel against God and the oppressor of men. In the end the teeth of this savage "lion" are broken, and he therefore starves to death, along with his children ("the whelps of the lioness")—a complete failure in the race of life. (Cf. Franz Delitzsch, *The Book of Job,* 2 vols. [Reprint ed. Grand Rapids: Eerdmans, 1949], vol. 1, pp. 91-92.)

Second, does the law of retribution and reward operate without delay or interference (of at least a temporary sort) from complicating factors, in order to exercise the faith of truly committed believers?

Third, does the law of retribution operate in such a direct and immediate fashion that one may derive from it the corollary that all misfortune (especially of the catastrophic kind that has overtaken Job) points to a prior sin or series of transgressions that has brought it on? "Remember now, who ever perished being innocent? Or where were the righteous destroyed?" (v. 7) strongly affirms this corollary. And yet it is hard to imagine that Eliphaz had never heard of the murder of Abel.

This dogmatic position on retribution, that calamity is never visited upon the innocent but only upon the guilty, furnishes a fundamental motif throughout the Book of Job, and therefore it requires careful examination. It was more than a mere theological interest that motivated these three visitors to go down to Uz and interview Job. It was in fact a matter of deep personal concern to them to establish some secret offense of a very grave nature as the real cause of Job's afflictions; otherwise the same nonretributive calamities might conceivably fall upon them as well. If Job was really as blameless and as holy as everyone had understood him to be prior to his terrible misfortunes, then what was there to prevent similar disaster from befalling them as well, no matter how godly their lives? This was an extremely disturbing case to them, and so they had to research it with great care. The reason, therefore, behind their persistent goading and badgering is their own existential concern for their future safety. Job simply *had* to have done something very wicked indeed; otherwise there was no security for them either in maintaining a God-fearing standard of life. It is important to understand, even at this early stage of our study, that what God condemned in 42:7 (where he says to Eliphaz, "My wrath is kindled against you and against your two friends, because you have not spoken of Me what is right!") is precisely this cruelly simplistic condemnation and vilification of Job—which so grievously misrepresented the real workings of

God's providence and developed into cruel abuse rather than loving consolation toward this victim of such terrible misfortune. Their errand of ostensible kindness therefore turned out to be the unkindest affliction with which Job had to deal, for it amounted to an attack upon his very integrity and his faith in God.

One further observation is in order before I conclude this initial discussion of this false and pernicious doctrine. By implication it renders suspect every hero of the faith who has gone through great though undeserved suffering, but endured in the cause of the Lord. In the judgment of the three, all such martyrs must have been guilty of some secret sin, and the whole list of afflicted saints referred to in Hebrews 11:36-38 would come under renewed scrutiny, to see what sins they must have committed in order to incur persecution and death. Hence we may not regard this dogma of the three counselors as a minor slip in technical theology; on the contrary, it militates against the soundness of God's government in administering the fortunes of His children on earth. By implication it even gives aid and comfort to Satan, with his analysis of self-interest as being the wellspring of all morality in fallen man. No room would be left for the nobility of self-sacrificing heroism; even a martyr's untimely death would have to be understood as retribution for some personal transgression, known perhaps to himself alone.

3. (4:12-21) Eliphaz now shifts from his incisive definition of the doctrine of retribution as the reason for calamity, and offers a mystically derived insight that came to him in a dream. A mysterious angelic spirit spoke to him one night during a troubled sleep, and solemnly affirmed that no mortal man could pass judgment upon God in the matter of His administration of justice. Even the mightiest angels are subject to His correction; how much more the human race, frail and perishable and limited as it is in understanding! The clear implication for Job is that he had best surrender to the wisdom and holy justice of God, and acknowledge humbly his own sin and guilt that brought his calamities upon him.

C. Eliphaz Exhorts Job to Repentance (5)

1. (5:1–7) Eliphaz describes the melancholy fate of fools who oppose God.

a. (:1) Eliphaz now appeals to the testimony of human experience and the insights of holy sages of olden times.

b. (:2) Resentment (*ka'aś;* "vexation, indignation") and anger (*qin'āh;* also translated as "envious zeal") toward God's standards and commandments lead only to the destruction of the fool (*'ewīl*) or simpleton (*pōteh;* a gullible dupe who believes the false promises of Satan) who imagines he can flout the moral law.

c. (:3–7) Even though such a self-willed rebel may appear to succeed at first, he labors under an inexorable curse, the blameful effects of which will blight his children. He may temporarily accumulate wealth, but he is destined to lose it to greedy and crafty foes. Nor may he assign his reverses to mere chance or bad luck ("affliction does not come from the dust," v. 6); it is rather because of evil self-assertion against God that men are prone to fall into trouble and distress. "For man is born for trouble, As sparks fly upward" (v. 7).

2. (5:8–16) Hope is in store for those who turn to God, the righteous judge who crushes the pride of the wicked.

a. (:8–9) "In your place, Job, I would commit all my sorrow and difficulty to our wonder-working God."

b. (:10–14) God rules over nature, so that rain waters the earth; He exalts the abased and safeguards those who mourn, yet overturns the schemes of crafty plotters and brings them to frustration and eventual failure. He even "captures the wise by their own shrewdness," (v. 13); that is, they are caught in the very trap they have laid for others (a verse that is quoted with approval in

I Corinthians 3:19). The point is, in the end the worldly-wise turn
out to be the eternal losers; it is hopeless to bet against God! They
end up by blindly stumbling about in the light of God's revealed
truth; they "grope at noon as in the night." This verse (14) was
later incorporated in the eloquent confession of national failure
and sin in Isaiah 59:10.

  c. (:15–16) But the poor who trust in God and follow Him are
delivered from the wealthy oppressor, and those who seem to
be in a hopeless plight find their hopes fulfilled by their faithful
God, who crushes the pretensions of the unscrupulous braggart.

  3. (5:17–27) Eliphaz describes the blessed state of the humble,
submissive believer.

  a. (:17) The chastening and reproof of a teachable believer is
really a blessing in disguise. (This verse is adopted and elaborated
in Proverbs 3:11–12, which is later quoted in Hebrews 12:5–6. It
contains a much-needed insight that applies to every generation.
Hebrews 12:11 gives it perhaps the finest formulation in all of
Scripture.)

  b. (:18–21) God is faithful in healing the wounds He inflicts on
His children, and in delivering them from those difficulties into
which He has brought them. He is educating them for spiritually
productive living here on earth and for heaven to come. In time of
famine and the dangers of war He knows how to deliver those
who trust and obey Him. He can even deliver them from those
slanders and injustices that are directed against the God-fearing
by others in their own community.

  c. (:22–25) The safety of the believer in time of danger or star-
vation is guaranteed. Not even the stones in his cultivated fields
(a real problem for farmers in Edom and North Arabia) will
prevent his crops from flourishing as they should ("You will be in
league with the stones of the field," v. 23), nor will the predatory

beasts prey upon his flocks and herds. His home will be secure from harm and his children will be many.

d. (:26–27) Such an obedient, humbly trusting servant of the Lord is sure to maintain his health until his dying day—as a seal of God's approval upon his faithfulness. Job should gratefully embrace this solid confidence in the trustworthiness of God's educative discipline and protective, fostering care. Eliphaz avers that he has learned this wonderful provision of God from both his own experience and his observation.

There are many reassurances in chapter 5 that are valid for the Christian who feels he is in serious difficulty or danger. In general the argument seems to approach the principle of God's loving, all-wise providence so beautifully set forth in Romans 8:28.

Yet Eliphaz's monologue suffers from one grave defect in that it misleads the Lord's disciple into supposing that he will be safe-guarded against the "slings and arrows of outrageous fortune" to an extent that would preclude the sufferings of a Job, a Jeremiah, a Stephen, or a Paul. In other words, it so overstates the case as to lend it a false rosy glow. Those true believers who find themselves afflicted beyond the implied limits of the idealistic description of verses 18–25 may well be driven to despair, for those verses seem to imply divine promises that are not actually fulfilled.

This pair of chapters (4–5) also adds up to one false insinuation that is directed unfairly against Job: that he must have been over-taken by the consequences of his own misdeeds. To get back into God's favor and to come under His gracious protection Job must confess what he has done amiss, and then he has only to pray the penitent's prayer and all will be well with him again. But what Eliphaz completely overlooks is the possibility that Job may never have committed any such grievous offenses as Eliphaz implies. He fails to see the gross injustice of imputing some secret wrongdoing to Job simply because he has been overtaken by devastating calamity. To make such an accusation (no matter how veiled and indirect it may be) without a scintilla of evidence is altogether indefensible.

D. Job's Remonstrance and Defense Against Eliphaz (6–7)

1. (6:1–7) Job explains why his language has been so extreme, but urges that his grounds for bitterness should be more fairly understood, and that he should not be fed with such tasteless counsel as Eliphaz has given him.

a. (:1–4) "Under the terrible pressure of my afflictions—much beyond anything you, Eliphaz, have ever known or could even imagine, I have been driven to express myself in rash and extreme language. But you must understand my ill-considered words in the light of the terrible stress to which I have been subjected. I have become virtually demoralized by the poisoned arrows that the Almighty (*Shaddai*) has shot into my soul, and the frightful losses and pain that He has inflicted upon me. Job seems to imply that those who have never gone through the experiences from which he now suffers can never properly appreciate the intensity of the anguish to the hapless victim—a consideration that should lead Eliphaz to something beyond mere sanctimonious moralizing.

b. (:5–7) "The patronizing advice, with its unfair insinuation that I have been hiding some secret, unconfessed sin, is as loathsome and tasteless as unsalted albumen of an egg."

2. (6:8–13) Job repeats his desire to be released by death, feeling that if death should come, he still has the satisfaction of knowing that through all his agonies he has never gone so far as to deny God or to spurn His Word. But since he has been so completely drained of his emotional stamina and strength, he might as well be cut off from this life, knowing that with God turned against him, he is completely without help or hope.

3. (6:14–23) Job expresses keen disappointment in the way these professed friends have betrayed him in his time of need.

1. (:14) These friends have failed to show even that basic ingredient of kindness that friendship should always include—the encouraging word that should help the wretched victim of misfortune to keep his grip on God. Job seems to imply here that Eliphaz's approach, no matter how kindly meant, has served more to alienate the sufferer from God—at least the kind of God Eliphaz believes in—than to draw him closer to Him.

b. (:15-20) Job has found these three friends, who at first seemed such a welcome balm to his beleaguered soul, to be a complete disappointment and frustration to him as soon as they opened their mouths to accuse him unjustly. Here he uses an analogy very appropriate for desert travelers like the Arabians, that is, the reference to a wadi or seasonal stream, which carries abundant water during the rainy season but dries up all too soon during the dry, hot months of the year. The thirsty traveler catches sight of it at a distance, and eagerly covers the intervening distance to find refreshment for his thirst. But when he reaches its banks he finds that even though there is still green shrubbery around the stream bed, all the water is gone. Even so the three counselors have given Job no comfort or relief but only the keenest disappointment. (Lord, grant that when troubled souls turn to us for comfort and counsel, they may find in us those rivers of living water that Jesus promised to those who have drunk deeply of Him [John 7:38].)

c. (:21-23) Job now observes that, whatever their announced motives may have been in visiting him, his counselors' ministry to him has proved to be a complete disappointment. Instead of sympathetic consolation and understanding they have reacted with alarm at seeing his plight and have turned out to be worse than useless. They should take due note of the fact that he has asked no financial favors or intervention with the government on his behalf.

4. (6:24-30) Job now faces Eliphaz squarely on the issue of fairness and justice in regard to his alleged sinfulness as the ground of his calamities.

a. (:24–26) Job says, "I now face you as a defendant in a court action, and I have a right to hear specific, documented charges, rather than mere inferences or surmises. Honest accusations I can appreciate, but never the vague insinuations you have leveled at me. All you have against me up until now, so far as I can see, are a few exaggerations and extreme terms I may have used in voicing my despair. But should these not be interpreted as an expression of anguished emotion, rather than as sober theological definitions?" In other words, no competent counselor should fail to make allowances for the language of overreaction from a victim of intense emotional or physical suffering. In such situations none of us says exactly what he means as he expresses how he feels. "Do you intend to reprove my words, when the words of one in despair belong to the wind?" (v. 26).

b. (:27–30) Job continues, "With an attitude like that, Eliphaz, you would show legalistic censoriousness even toward a hapless orphan if you would thus deal with a friend of longstanding (like myself). Now give me an honest appraisal; deal with me as a person rather than a mere pawn for your dogmatic inferences. If you can find no falsehood or injustice in my words, then it is unjust for you to presume that there is dishonesty in my heart." This comes quite close to the legal maxim: The accused is presumed to be innocent until proven guilty.

Job adds, "Just look me in the eye, Eliphaz, and carefully, fairly examine me with probing questions, and then see if you can detect any falsehood in me. Otherwise, stop badgering me and accept me as honest and sincere when I tell you I have done nothing that I am concealing."

5. (7:1–10) Job appeals to the three for kindness, on the ground of his unremitting illness and the swift approach of a death that will forever remove him from their eyes.

a. (:1–6) "We mortals are like hardworking day laborers who perform their drudgery for a meager stipend. And in my case the weeks and months go by with unremitting pressure, such that all day long I yearn for the night to come. And then when it arrives, I toss and turn, unable to rest or sleep, and long for the dawn to break. Thus day and night alternate like a weaver's shuttle at the loom; and yet it all goes on in complete futility, without any hope of deliverance or amendment." Nothing is so depressing as an illness that never diminishes or allows any hope of cure. This serves to erode all the fortitude and stamina with which the sufferer first began his trial.

b. (:7–10) "As you deal with this broken wreck of a man, please remember that I am not going to be around very much longer, with my hopeless and incurable disease. And consider also that when I am gone and leave this earth behind as I descend to Sheol, I will never return, and you will not have to bother with me any more." This is a truly pathetic appeal to Job's three friends for a little more consideration and pity, and a little less tormenting with false accusations of evil.

6. (7:11–21) Turning from the unjust suspicions of his human companions, Job appeals directly to God, pleading for relief from his nightmarish existence and at least some brief intervals of surcease from his unremitting torment.

a. (:11–19) To God, who really understands him and knows the truth about him, Job feels he can pour out his anguish and bitter complaint, without being cruelly misinterpreted (as he has been by his human counselors). "Lord," he protests, "why do you guard me in the cage of affliction so diligently, as if I were some dangerous monster? Why do you constantly afflict me with horrible nightmares whenever I try to sleep? Why can't you let me have a little relief once in a while and just leave me alone so I can catch my breath and swallow my saliva?"

b. (:20–21) Job now appeals earnestly to God to show him whatever he may have done to bring on these calamities. If only He would let him know why he has been set up as a target for all those arrows of misfortune that have so grievously wounded him! This was one of the most galling features of Job's tribulation: that he could find not the slightest clue for God's fierce wrath against him. The most shattering feature for Job was his feeling that God no longer loved him or cared about him, except to crush him with misfortune. He couldn't think of anything he had done that could have changed God's attitude toward him so drastically.

In closing, Job beseeches God to show him just a little mercy before he dies. Whatever he may have done amiss, cannot the Lord find it in His heart to forgive him—especially since he does not know what his sin was, or he would confess it and repent of it—and pardon his transgression before his miserable earthly existence comes to an end? Nothing could be more heart-rending than such anguished appeals on the part of a sincere believer who has always followed the Lord. But they fail to move the compassions of a dogmatician like Bildad, as we shall see.

E. Bildad's Rejoinder to Job: Your Sniveling Complaints Impugn the Justice of God and Attack the Foundations of the Moral Order! (8)

1. (8:1–7) "You are only getting what you deserve," Bildad tells Job, "for charging God with injustice instead of suing Him for mercy!"

a. (:1–3) "Your complaints imply that God perverts justice, and this is nothing short of blasphemy!"

b. (:4) "Not even you can deny that your children sinned against the Lord and He made them suffer the consequences." It should be noted that this was a most callous and unfeeling way for Bildad to assume from their sudden death that Job's children all had been

guilty of mortal sin. He had no certain knowledge that this was
so, and it was cruel of him thus gratuitously to vilify their
memory, without a single expression of sympathy or regret.

   c. (:5-7) "If you are as blameless as you claim to be, then all you
have to do is pray for God's mercy and kindness, and He will
surely deliver you from your plight. It is as simple as that! And
then your future will brighten up and you will end up with
prosperity and success once again."

   2. (8:8-10) "Consider carefully the accumulated wisdom of our
forefathers in generations past, remembering that we in our own
short lifetime can never hope to equal or surpass them in insight.
Just listen to what they have to tell you about the laws of failure
and success."

   3. (8:11-20) "There is a clear principle of cause and effect in this
world, such that from an effect one can validly deduce what its
cause must have been."

   a. (:11-14) "Just as papyrus and reeds infallibly indicate marshy
ground covered with water, and are both of them subject to
withering more quickly than plants that are grown on a normal
field, so also is the self-confident man who ignores God and then
finds all his hopes of success are dashed to the ground."

   b. (:15-18) "Such a man's reliance on material values and an
earthly home will prove to be vain, despite his brief prosperity, for
it has no foundation in the Lord. In the end he will vanish from
that world which he chose in preference to God, and will leave no
mark of achievement or honor in it."

   c. (:19-20) "A self-seeking materialist is doomed to futility precisely because of the righteous judgment of God, who never casts
off or rejects a sincere servant of His (as He has evidently done

with you), and who never upholds the evildoer, even though he may at first seem successful (as you were)."

4. (8:21–22) "Therefore it is the result of this trial that will demonstrate your integrity and shame your detracters and foes (that is, *if* indeed you are innocent!)."

Here we see that Bildad, in a way even more direct and simplistic than that of Eliphaz, bases Job's exoneration completely on the objective evidence of material success. As we have already observed, this excludes the faith-testing kind of trial that God has appointed for Job. The irony of Bildad's professed zeal to uphold God's honor and justice is that he squarely sets himself against the will and plan of God, and puts himself uncomfortably close to agreeing with Satan that the real basis for human virtue is enlightened self-interest.

F. Job's Response to Bildad: No Mortal Man May Argue
His Innocence Before the Almighty; Yet He May
Protest Against Cruelly Unfair Treatment (9–10)

1. (9:1–12) "There is no way in which any man, even if innocent, could plead his cause before the omnipotent sovereign of the universe, and so no vindication is possible."

a. (:1–4) "How could any human complainant, even one who is blameless, ever bring the Almighty into court in order to set forth the merits of his case, since His power is irresistible even before the bar of absolute justice?"

b. (:5–10) "Our God is sovereign over all the starry heavens, and master over sky and sea. How then can any creature call Him to account for anything He does, or defend his own cause before Him?"

c. (:11–12) "Since He is invisible, there is no way I can face Him with my complaint; no one can call Him to account, no matter what or whom He chooses to snatch away."

   2. (9:13-24) "It would be impossible to secure redress from Him if I am innocent and my cause is just; He can destroy the righteous as well as the wicked, with no one to call Him into court."

   a. (:13–15) "How could I plead my cause before the Most High, who overthrew even the power of Egypt ("the helpers of Rahab," v. 13) in the days of Moses, even if I were in the right? Before such an adversary in court I would encounter my divine judge, and could only cast myself upon His mercy."

   b. (:16–20) "After He has crushed and wounded me for no known reason, I could hardly believe He was answering me, if afterward He should choose to do so. Tormented as I am, I would surely be speechless before Him, even if I could confront Him, and though I were innocent, I would be guilty of presumption even to offer my defense before Him, who is beyond the jurisdiction of any court."

   c. (:21–24) "Although I am actually not at fault, it makes no difference; my freedom from blame, or even my life itself, is of no account before Him, for He allows wickedness to prevail on earth and judgment to be withheld by the judges who are bound to administer it. Or at least, so it appears, since these injustices are allowed to continue even though He is able to enforce the right."
   It should be observed that Job in his willingness to lay the blame for injustice upon the negligence or callousness of the Lord, simply upon the basis of appearances, incurs the guilt of presumptuously condemning the Lord who is Himself the source of all moral awareness in man. For this he later will be rebuked roundly by both Elihu and Yahweh Himself. He is particularly at fault for imputing to God an indifference to injustice by men toward one another and an attitude of mockery toward its

victims—a slanderous misrepresentation of the holiness of God. Yet this bitter conclusion, drawn from his own unexplained afflictions, did not represent his real, underlying trust in the wisdom and righteousness of God as expressed later in his debate with the three. Compare, for example, 19:25.

3. (9:25-35) "My helplessness before Him renders my swiftly passing days full of futility and despair, unless some umpire could intervene to bring God and me together for a settlement of my case."

a. (:25-29) "If I should try to take my mind off of my present woes, and face my swiftly speeding days with manly cheerfulness, I know full well that periods of agonizing pain will still overtake me, and my bravest efforts will be useless."

b. (:30-31) "No matter how completely I might exonerate myself ("wash myself with snow And cleanse my hands with lye," v. 30), my divine adversary would so utterly pollute me with the guilt of presumption—for I may not answer Him the way I could with some human litigant—that I would have to condemn me myself."

c. (:32-35) "The problem is that there is no umpire or arbitrator (*mōwkīªḥ;* one who comes to a verdict after hearing both sides and then pronounces the appropriate sentence) between us. For unless the Lord withholds His ceaseless rod of affliction, there is no way that I can frame an answer before Him."

Here we see that Job's protest is based upon the inherent and essential unfairness of the position in which he is placed, because He who should be his judge and guarantor of justice has actually become his adversary and persecutor, apparently without cause—certainly without any cause known to Job.

4. (10:1-7) Job earnestly remonstrates with God for treating him as a suspect to be investigated for a crime, when He actually knows that Job is innocent.

a. *(:1–3)* "But regardless of imperiling my own safety (for what more do I have to fear than what has already befallen me?) I will voice my complaint to Thee, O Lord, with all the resentment of my heart. For Thou hast turned against me for no reason at all, and apparently condemned me when I have done nothing to deserve it. How canst Thou smile upon the schemes of the wicked?"

b. *(:4–7)* "But how canst Thou deal thus with me, when Thou seest all the facts as they are, rather than needing to investigate and find out the truth, as mere human prosecutors have to do? Knowing full well that I am innocent, why dost Thou not deliver me from my distress and disgrace?"

5. (10:8–17) It is the Lord who fashioned him, Job reminds Him; but after showing him such loving-kindness in earlier life, how can He so unrelentingly reduce him to misery and disgrace, and allow these false witnesses to badger him?

a. *(:8–12)* With the loving care of a father concerned for his little one, God carefully fashioned his body and watched over the welfare of his body and soul—until now!

b. *(:13–17)* Yet with all this kindness and care, the Lord secretly prepared this final tribulation, regardless of whether Job committed evil (for which he would be held inexorably accountable) or remained innocent. Even then disgrace and misery were to be his portion, and now he is hunted down like a lion's prey, and harassed by these three men who unfairly accuse him of things he never did, as they watch him being assailed by one tribulation after another.

Note that in this chapter also Job clearly accuses God of cruel unfairness and injustice—judging entirely from appearances alone, without considering that God might have some good and sufficient reason that Job knows nothing about.

6. (10:18-22) Job makes a closing appeal to the Lord for a little relief before he departs this life for a land beyond the grave, shrouded in darkness and gloom.

a. (:18-19) Why didn't God let him die as an infant? That would have been much kinder than the way his long life has turned out.

b. (:20-22) After all Job has been through, why can't the Lord let him have just a little release from anguish before he passes out into the night on his dying day? To Job in his present mood, it seems that the world beyond is enveloped in murky darkness. (Contrast his earlier description of it in 3:17-19 as a land of rest, freedom, and peace.)

G. *Zophar's Response to Job: God Is Right*
   and You Are Wrong! Better Get Right with Him,
   for the Wicked Are Without Hope (11)

1. (11:1-6) "You have been most eloquent on your own behalf, Job, declaiming boastfully of your blamelessness, but if God should reveal what He knows about your sin, it would then be a different story! You have received only half the punishment you deserved!"

2. (11:7-12) "Your finite mind cannot possibly fathom the wisdom of the Almighty, deeper than Sheol and loftier than the heavens, and broader than the ocean itself. No one can set limits to His power or deceive Him as to what iniquity he has done (as Job thinks he can!). But Job is a spiritual idiot, who can no more gain wisdom than a donkey can give birth to a man."

3. (11:13-20) Zophar makes an altar call: "If only you would turn back to God in full repentance and put away your sin, then you would enter into a new state of peace and power, of security and blessing under God, and others would turn to you for counsel

and help. But stubborn refusal to repent and confess can lead to
no other outcome but death in the case of the sinner."

In this short rebuke and exhortation we see the severe Zophar
attempting to force Job to admit his hidden transgressions, on the
basis of a glowing account of the rich benefits accruing from
repentance and new surrender to God. Then, of course, he and
his two comrades can go home relieved at the confirmation of
their doctrine that disaster will never overtake truly good
people—like themselves!

Now that all three counselors have made their contribution,
largely agreeing with each other that Job's basic problem is some
hidden and unconfessed sin that he needs to reveal before man
and God as he humbly repents of it, in order that God may relieve
him of illness and restore him to favor once more, Job is ready to
give them a general response, rather than reply to Zophar's
remarks alone. He therefore tells them that their platitudes and
generalities about the greatness and goodness of God are conven-
tional sentiments that he also could express, yet they throw but
little light and afford absolutely no comfort at all on his own
desperate plight. Their stereotyped formula of cause accurately
inferrable from effect has led them to cruel and unfeeling
judgmentalism—as indeed it has.

H. *Job Answers His Accusers (12–14)*

Job continues, "In your smug self-satisfaction you have mocked
me with your hackneyed maxims and unfeeling contempt, and so
I turn from you to God as He really is, in all His greatness and
glory, rather than to your limited concept of Him. It may be that
He will hear my cry and understand me, even though you do not."

1. (12:1–6) "In your pompous pride you feel you have attained
the ultimate in wisdom, as you mouth your trite generalizations
(which I could frame as well as you) and subject me to derision
and contempt as a true servant of God, even while you remain
oblivious to the secure prosperity of many who are evildoers in

this present evil world, and make a god of their own right hand."
(Note this rendering of the final clause in NIV: "those who carry
their god in their hands"—rather than taking ${}^\prime El\bar{o}{}^a h$ ["God"] as the
subject of the verb $h\bar{e}b\hat{\imath}{}^\prime$ ["has brought into"] as the NASB does
with its "Whom God brings into his power"—a rendering that is
grammatically possible but does not fit the context as well.)

2. (12:7–12) And yet it remains true that the Lord God is indeed
worthy of all the thanksgiving and praise that ascends to Him
from the beasts and the birds and even the fish of the sea for the
gift of life; for they all are aware of this just as much as the three
sages profess to be (on the basis of the excellent pronouncements
made by wise men of old, men who acquired much insight as long
as they lived. "Wisdom is with aged men, With long life is understanding," v. 12). Here Job shows a due appreciation for the
wisdom they all have inherited from the past—even though Bildad
(8:8–10) had implied that he had turned his back upon the
ancients.

3. (12:13–25) God is in very truth the all-wise sovereign over
the forces of nature (controlling both flood and drought) and over
the leaders of men as well, for He governs with irresistible
strength and surpassing wisdom (v. 16—$t\bar{u}^w shiyy\bar{a}h$, i.e., practical,
effective wisdom that achieves results).

a. (:17–21) God humbles human counselors, judges, and kings
by reducing them to dishonor and defeat; likewise priests and
nobles and champion warriors. All the great ones of earth are as
nothing before Him.

b. (:22–25) God is the revealer of mysteries as well (a sentiment
echoed in Daniel 2:22 after the disclosure of Nebuchadnezzar's
fateful dream), and the controller of the destinies of nations as
they rise and fall, while their befuddled leaders are no longer able
to keep them from ruin.

4. (13:1–12) These three worthless physicians will only incur God's wrath rather than His favor, as they unfairly distort the evidence in His favor (—a prediction that was fulfilled later in 42:7ff.), as if He needed their biased defense of His providential dealings. "On the contrary, He will roundly condemn you for dishonesty, and your sententious judgments as worthless, brittle clay."

5. (13:13–28) Job now appeals directly to God to hear his case and show him what he may have done amiss.

a. (:13–15) Forbidding the three counselors to interrupt him, Job turns from their heartless incomprehension to cast himself directly upon God, even if he forfeits his life in the process (v. 15).[2]

b. (:16–19) Job is willing to risk annihilation by God for presuming to argue his case directly before Him—a destruction that would surely follow if he came before Him with a guilty heart. In that case Job would drop dead and the whole matter would be settled beyond all human jurisdiction.

c. (:20–28) As he thus approaches God directly, Job begs for a fair hearing before an adversary who is at the same time his divine judge.

---

2. Note that NASB and NIV support KJV in rendering *Hēn yiqṭᵉlēnīy lōʾ ᵃyaḥēl* as "though He slay me, I will trust in Him." RSV renders the phrase as "Behold, he will slay me; I have no hope," which would, apart from the context, be the normal and obvious way to translate these four words. But the *hēn* here should be taken as the word *if* or *though*, a meaning it normally bears in Aramaic. However, it is used the same way only in Hebrew poetry. Secondly, the word *lōʾ*, "not," may have been miscopied from *lōw*, "in Him." These homonyms were quite often confused by the copyists, and the Massoretes show this correction here in the margin of their text. The RSV rendering cannot be reconciled successfully with verse 14, which certainly suggests that Job did have some hope that God would hear him and vindicate him. Nor can it lead into verse 16, which holds out the prospect of Job's success in this direct appeal.

First Job pleads for the withholding of two possible barriers to his presenting his case: the paralyzing effect of standing directly in God's presence, even though that presence was unseen, with the result that he could not articulate his defense; and the suppressing power of God's almighty hand, which would utterly crush him before he could even begin his defense (vv. 20–21).

Next Job implores God—even though He is unseen—to give him a hearing as he speaks, and then to respond to him and let him know what the facts are, as God Himself perceives them (v. 22).

Third, Job beseeches the Lord to tell him why He has become alienated from him and taken him to be His enemy rather than His loving servant. Why has He directed such terrible punishment against a frail and helpless person like himself, a mere "driven leaf" or a piece of "dry chaff" (vv. 24–25)?

In His indictment against Job, does He include those sins he committed long ago as a callow youth—sins that were repented of, confessed, and completely forsaken (v. 26)?

If it is not for these, why has He treated Job like a condemned felon, rotting away with his feet in the stocks (vv. 27–28)?

6. (14:1–12) Job expresses the pathos of the human experience: his life is so short and his death is so final.

a. (:1–4) Man is really a pathetic figure, with a lifetime so brief (almost like a flower's), so subject to trouble, so prone to fall under the condemnation of his Maker because of sin, and so inclined to commit sin because of his essential impurity.

b. (:5–6) In view of man's transiency and frailty, would it not be appropriate for the Lord to look less rigorously upon his errors and let him stumble his way without undue harassment to his speedy end?

c. (:7–12) In the vegetable kingdom there is a prospect of physical regeneration and renewal, as the felled tree sends up fresh shoots; but this is not so with the human race. Once his body is lowered into the grave, a man never rises or survives in any physical fashion, any more than evaporated water from rivers or seas ever returns in the form of its parent bodies (except indirectly, as raindrops resulting from the precipitation cycle).

7. (14:13–22) In his present state of affliction and unremitting persecution under the wrath of God, Job would much prefer to be hidden away in Sheol (the realm of the dead) rather than go on as now, with all earthly hopes destroyed. Better to depart for the life beyond than to decline into marred appearance and senile preoccupation with his own aches and pains.

a. (:13–17) But even though the buried corpse can never be revived, yet it is much better to leave this life and be sheltered in the refuge of Sheol, until at length God's wrath against him would be fully spent and He would feel sorry and lonesome for Job, as one whom He fashioned for Himself. As for Job's physical death, it will mean the discharge from his harsh military service (his *ṣābā'*—which means either "army" or "army service"), at the conclusion of which his *ḥᵃlīpāh* ("change" or "release" or even "renewal") comes to him—that is, the release from the burdens and anxieties of this earthly life in order to retire into the quiet and peace of the life beyond (3:17–19). After God's indignation against him has spent itself, surely He will want His chastened, much afflicted child back again, and his sins will be covered over and sealed up in the bag of forgetfulness. (NIV's rendering here is much to be preferred: "My offenses will be sealed up in a bag; you will cover over my sin.")

From the context it seems beyond question that the intent of verse 14—"If a man dies, will he live again?"—is not to deny resurrection or the survival of the soul after the interment of the body, but only to rule out physical resuscitation. That this query is immediately followed by a reference to his "change" or "release" is proof positive that Job understood that upon death he would in his soul be transferred from earthly life to a continuing existence in the life beyond, with a comforting possibility of renewed fellow-ship with the Lord at that time. Despite much learned discussion encountered in some of the commentaries, no other interpretation of verse 14 does justice to the rights of language.

b. (:18–22) But here in this present life as the years pass by, our bodies gradually wear out, like mountains eroded by rushing streams, and the infirmities of old age take the chief attention of the decaying retiree, even as his appearance declines into the ugliness of decrepitude. Finally he even loses interest in the success or progress of his children and he becomes preoccupied with his own aches and pains.

In his present melancholy situation Job cannot help viewing the whole process of life as a depressing experience, hardly worth prolonging into extreme old age. But very clearly he shows a hope of a tranquil and sheltered continuation of life beyond the grave.

III. The Debate Continued: The Second Cycle (15–21)

A. Eliphaz Accuses Job of Presumption in Disregarding the Wisdom of the Ancients and Criticizing God As Unjust (15)

1. (15:1–6) "Job, your long-winded arguments are full of empty eloquence and fury, but they signify nothing that is valid and sound—only that which undermines true faith and casts reproach upon God. Your very language before us is sufficient to condemn you, even apart from your sins of the past."

2. (15:7–16) "You talk as if you have lived longer and learned more than all the great sages of the past. What makes you think that you are wiser than we or the older thinkers in our own day? Why are you not content with the comforting promises of God to repentant sinners? How can you presume to turn against Him with indignation and resentment? How can you imagine that any member of our fallen race may challenge the justice of Him who is too holy. and pure to accept even the angels themselves as free from blame? How much less will He acquit an evil-loving, detestable, corrupt sinner like you!"

Thus it has become apparent that the kindly, solicitous counselor of chapter 4 was really playing a role that he can no longer maintain in the face of vigorous disagreement. At this stage his language becomes almost abusive, and he is ready to believe all evil of anyone who would try to refute him in argument.

3. (15:17-26) Eliphaz now declares what sages of the past discovered and taught to the forefathers concerning the troubles and terrors that beset the ungodly and ruthless sinner, who can expect no future but darkness, danger, and anguish that will overwhelm him, even as he shakes his puny fist against the Almighty in an absurd attempt to overthrow His power on earth.

4. (15:27-35) The fleeting success and prosperous fatness of the self-willed rebel against God will give way to ruined fortunes and wretched penury, for he cannot escape the sure vengeance of the Almighty. He will at last discover that his trust in vanity and violence has led him only to ruin and loss, and all his achievements will be consumed by the flames of God's judgment.

Since Eliphaz makes no mention of retribution after death, he seems to imply that all the wicked will surely suffer their just deserts in this life and suffer all the dreadful consequences of their sins before they die. In this respect Eliphaz shows himself to be out of touch with reality—as Job later points out to him in 21:7-13 and elsewhere.

B. *Job's Reply to Eliphaz: It Is Easy to Berate a Victim*
   of Misfortune; Nevertheless I Will Appeal to God
   from My Unjust Accusers, For He Is
   My Last Resort (16–17)

1. (16:1–5) What wretched comforters to pass judgment against
the afflicted and helpless! It is easy for anyone to accuse, but a
true comforter will solace rather than plague his friend still further.
Note how important it is for counselors to avoid being judgmental
toward those they are supposed to be helping. The counselee
should always be made to feel that the counselor cares for him
and is on his side.

2. (16:6–17) "My agony is not lessened either by my speaking or
by my keeping silent.[1] God has worn me out, devastated my
household,[2] and reduced me to skin and bones."

a. (:7–9) "I am at a disadvantage from the outset as I try to plead
my cause, for my gaunt and wasted appearance makes me look
like a target of God's displeasure, ravaged and torn by my divine
adversary."

b. (:10–14) "Taking advantage of my helplessness, the human
onlookers have ganged up against me like a bunch of brutal
ruffians, for they can see how God suddenly plunged me from
secure prosperity into ruin and made me a target of His arrows,

1. NIV is to be preferred for verse 6b: "and if I refrain, it [my pain] does not go
away." NASB says, "And if I hold back, what has left me?" This translation doesn't
make much sense in this context. The Hebrew says literally, ". . . what goes from
me?"—that is, "departs from me."

2. Here again the NIV is to be preferred: "You have devastated my entire
household"—even though NASB's translation of "company" is technically correct
for *'ādāh* ("congregation; assembly; company"). In the light of Job's cultural setting,
the term *household* is appropriate for the entire population of Job's estate, including
family and servants of every description. The word *company* might suggest to the
modern reader a commercial corporation.

so that my wounded body pours forth its 'gall' upon the ground"
(perhaps an allusion to the constant oozing from his many sores).

c. (:15–17) "As a result of the assaults of God and men I must
clothe myself in sackcloth (or burlap) and plunge my face to the
ground (like a fallen bull whose horn—qeren—is jabbed into the
ground, v. 15), while my face is streaked with tears of helplessness
and frustration. Yet I have done nothing to deserve this maltreatment, for I have committed no violence or wrong to others."

Here again we see how Job misjudges the Lord, attributing to
Him causeless hostility or malice, as if He, rather than Satan,
were the occasion of his afflictions. In his extreme depression, Job
could only think that God, as absolute sovereign in the affairs of
men, must be responsible for it all. This failure of trust in God's
love is later sternly rebuked by Elihu; and indeed it constitutes a
genuine offense against the Lord on Job's part. On the other
hand, Job's mood and viewpoint changed from resentment and
reproach to an exalted conviction that despite all of his present
woe he will yet establish loving communication with Yahweh
once more, and the God of truth and justice will vindicate him in
the end. It should be clearly understood in this connection that
Job was not only concerned with personal vindication. More
importantly, he hoped that God might vindicate Himself in all His
faithfulness and integrity. Job could not bear the thought of God's
proving untrue to Himself!

3. (16:18–22) With all the intensity of his being Job implores the
earth not to "cover his blood" (i.e., allow him to be an unavenged
and unvindicated victim of injustice), and he beseeches heaven
that somehow he might get through to God before he dies in his
misery, and obtain a hearing through his heavenly advocate
(mēlîṣ—an interpreter who serves as an intermediary or ambassa-
dor). Despite the apparent hopelessness of his case, then, this
valiant loner refuses to give himself over to complete despair.
This is an important aspect of the true-to-life cycle of hope and
discouragement through which Job passed during these debates

with his friends. He expresses a sort of intuition that already there is an advocate (v. 19) pleading on his behalf before the throne of God—as if he somehow anticipated the glorious assurance of Hebrews 7:25 even before the first advent of Christ.

4. (17:1-5) Job renews his direct appeal to God to grant him a kind and just hearing, in contrast to the cruel mockery and self-serving denunciation that his human counselors have directed against him.

a. (:1-2) As Job teeters on the brink of death from his incurable illness he meets only with derision and hostility on the part of his friends.

b. (:3-5) If it is a bail or surety that Job needs in order to proceed with his case, only God can furnish such, since those in his audience have completely closed minds and damn him as guilty simply because of his sore affliction—and also because they think to obtain for themselves the reward of God's protection against any such disasters ever coming into their own lives.

5. (17:6-9) Job expresses the hope that even though he is now the butt of ridicule and shame as passers-by deride him in his deep melancholy and grief—so that upright men are now appalled at this strange misfortune that has overtaken him, and wonder at the apparent miscarriage of justice—yet the godly will persist in their loyal adherence to the standards of holiness and somehow grow stronger in their faithfulness to principle.

6. (17:10-16) Undaunted by his apparently hopeless plight, Job nevertheless challenges his critics to continue their shortsighted assaults against his integrity.

a. (:10-12) Job rejects as completely unfounded the false hope of recovery that the three had held out to him in their "altar-call" appeals for his repentance; they vainly "make night into day"

(v. 12), since no such repentance is possible for one like himself who has no secret transgressions to repent of.

b. (:13–16) As matters now stand (apart, of course, from the mediatorship of the advocate referred to in 16:19), Job has no hope at all but descent into Sheol, while his body molders in the grave. This statement ends with a touch of pathos as he asks, "Shall we—my hope (*tiqwāh*) and I—go down to the gates of Hades together?" Sheol seems to be considered here as a place of rest, at least of surcease from suffering and affliction, even if it would involve a failure on Job's part to achieve earthly vindication.

C. *Bildad's Reply to Job's Rejection: This Man Is Simply Receiving His Just Deserts (18)*

1. (18:1–4) "Job has cut off meaningful communication with us by his lack of understanding and his rejection of his friends as mere stupid beasts. He seems to think that if he is angry enough, he can alter the realities of this world and make it over into what he wants it to be; the earth to be abandoned and the rocks to be moved from their places!"

2. (18:5–14) Now comes a lurid description of the progressive involvement in calamitous misfortune that awaits the wicked man, as darkness closes in on him, his feet become entangled in a snare, and he finds himself surrounded by terrors on every side. At last he is dragged to his doom by the "king of terrors" (*melek ballāhôt,* verse 14, an obvious reference to Satan himself).

3. (18:15–21) Not only is the evildoer himself destroyed, but also his house and family are completely wiped out. The fire of destruction destroys his tent and sulphur is sprinkled over the ground on which he dwelt, and all memory of him perishes from the earth. Nor does he have any descendants to carry on his name, and all his neighbors to the east and west are utterly appalled at his lamentable and disgraceful end.

Thus Bildad is driven in the heat of the argument to conclude the worst about Job, since he has stubbornly refused to repent or fall in line with the pattern of contrition, sin-confession, and reformation in his conduct, as he has been urged to do. Bildad has turned a deaf ear to all of Job's protests of innocence, and he has firmly concluded from Job's unwillingness to repent that he must have a lot of repenting to do.

D. Job Responds to Bildad's Tirade with a Strong Appeal to God (19)

1. (19:1-6) "How heartless of you 'friends' to launch repeated attacks and reproaches against me, as you contemptuously look down upon me in my misery. Yet my wretched condition is a matter between me and God with which you have nothing to do (since, of course, you can point to no known transgression that I have committed, and have no basis for your charges)."

2. (19:7-12) "In my sorry plight I have not only received no redress or release from violence, but He Himself has hemmed me in with affliction and shut me up to despair as He allows me to be buffeted and besieged by His agents."

3. (19:13-22) "Because of His disfavor, my brothers and all my good friends, even the servants in my own home, have lost all care for me and turned their backs on me. None of them answers to my call and they all find me abhorrent—even the little children who mock at my affliction and my old comrades who now loathe me. In my utterly forsaken, lonely condition how can it be that you three cannot pity me as I groan in misery under the terrible misfortunes God has sent against me?"

Here Job expresses the full poignancy of utter loneliness before all human society, with all of his friends and dear ones turned against him, and concludes from his misfortunes that he is hated

and rejected even by God. Thus Job was suffering the utter for-
sakenness and contempt that the Servant of Jehovah ws later to
endure, according to Isaiah 53:3: "He was despised and forsaken
of men . . . And like one from whom men hide their face, He was
despised, and we did not esteem Him." Even his feeling of abandonment by God was to find a correspondence in Christ's cry of
dereliction upon the cross (Matt. 27:46). And yet, again like Jesus,
this sensation of abandonment by God the Father was succeeded
by a commitment of faith that transcended all adverse appearances. Job's "Nevertheless I know that my Redeemer liveth" (v. 25)
corresponds to Christ's "Father, into Thy hands I commit My
spirit!"

4. (19:23–24) Despite all of the condemnation Job receives from
his family and friends and the entire community that had so
highly honored him during his former days of prosperity, he
knows in his heart that he is innocent of any crime to account for
all his disasters. Therefore he wishes to write his averment of
guiltlessness upon a scroll of testimony, or better yet, incise it on
stone in letters filled in with lead (to preserve their legibility): "I,
Job, do solemnly aver that I have committed no such transgression
as to warrant the catastrophe that has befallen me!"

It should be noted that this reference to Job's ability to read and
write in his own language, which modern scholars used to insist
was impossible for the pre-Mosaic period, except perhaps for
a few professional scribes, has been proven possible by the
seventeenth-century B.C. West Semitic inscriptions discovered at
Serabit el-Khadim, in the Sinai Peninsula, where the Egyptians
used Semitic slaves to mine their turquoise for them. If even
slaves, belonging to the lowest social stratum, were thus capable
of reading and writing in their own language as well as Egyptian,
then it is absurd to deny this literacy to Job and his peers in the
leading classes of North Arabic and Edomite society. Therefore
we may understand this reference to Job's knowledge of writing
as historically credible.

5. (19:25–27) Yet even apart from such written affirmation, Job has someone far more decisive to vindicate his character: his kinsman-redeemer (gōʾēl) is God Himself, his ever-living witness and defender who will some day stand upon this earth and declare his innocence. Note that Job was not as concerned about the vindication of his own honor as he was about the honor of God Himself; for it would turn out to be a reproach against the Lord's integrity if He were to allow such gross injustice to befall an innocent man without ever exonerating him!

But when does Job expect God to appear on earth as his Redeemer? Not until after Job has died, and after the worms have eaten away his skin and flesh within the tomb (v. 26). Even after that has happened Job expects to see the Lord appear on his behalf. This can only mean that Job understood that he himself would live on, even after his body had died. No annihilation, no soul-sleep! His soul would keep right on in conscious existence—a testimony that should be borne in mind whenever certain scholars try to maintain that Old Testament believers had no notion of immortality.

Furthermore, Job was confident of seeing the Lord *from* (*min*) his resurrection body. Some Bible translations (including even NASB) translate 19:26b as, "Yet without my flesh I shall see God." But this interpretation violates all parallel usage of the verb *to see* (ḥāzāh, or even its synonym, rāʾāh) when used with the preposition *min* ("from"). In some contexts *min* may mean "without," but never with the verb *to see*. Always *min* indicates the vantage point from which the seeing or viewing is done. Therefore we must adopt the KJV rendering, "yet in my flesh I shall see God," which is followed by the NIV as well. If then Job is going to see God *from* his flesh, or physical body, he must have understood by this a body in which his soul or spirit would dwell after his first body had moldered away in the grave. And so here we have the doctrine of the bodily resurrection implied even in the first written book of the Old Testament!

Verse 27 reiterates this uplifting confidence: "He whom I shall behold for myself, and my eyes shall see, rather than any stranger (for $w^e l\bar{o}'$ $z\bar{a}r$)." Most translators take $z\bar{a}r$ as a second subject to $r\bar{a}'\bar{u}^w$, "see," rather than its object. But it provides fewer problems to take $z\bar{a}r$, "a stranger," as object of the verb. In other words, the God whom Job expects to behold in his resurrection body will be no stranger to him, but rather the faithful, redeeming God whom he has always known. And then, appropriately enough, Job exclaims in eager anticipation: "How my heart yearns (*kilyōtay kālū*^{w}—"my kidneys waste away") within me."

6. (19:28–29) Job closes with a warning to those who are trying to hound him to death by their constant harassment, accusing him of heinous guilt, that they themselves will have to fear the punishment of the Lord for their injustice and cruelty toward a victim of misfortune.

E. Zophar Replies That Job Has Rejected God Himself
by Criticizing His Administration of Justice (20)

1. (20:1–11) Surely Job should know what all of past history testifies, that the happiness of a wrongdoer comes finally to a sudden end, and his pride will be completely abased. He will be so completely swept away that he will leave nothing behind him, and his children will have to surrender all his wealth to the poor.

2. (20:12–19) The pleasure that the wicked man derives from his knavery will soon give way to bitter retribution, and he will have to give up all of his ill-gotten gain as he discovers that all of his gains have led only to dreadful loss. His deprivation of the poor will result in his own impoverishment.

3. (20:20–29) The wicked man's insatiable craving for ever more riches will result only in a loss of all his prosperity and abundance, and he will find himself a hapless fugitive from the avenging arrows of God. The fire of divine judgment will consume his household as the shame of his guilt is uncovered before the world.

Here again we see how unrelenting was the fanatical hostility aroused by Job's refusal to confess to sins he never committed.

F. Job Counters with a Challenge to Zophar
That He Is Out of Touch with Reality;
Not All Injustices Are Righted in This Life (21)

1. (21:1-16) "Honesty demands our facing the fact (though you may scoff at this) that punishment does not always overtake the wicked. Some of them enjoy prosperity, large families, freedom from fear, music and dancing, and they even go down to the grave in peace, after cynically scorning God to their dying day—and that too by His tolerance of their wicked ways!"

What Job brings out here certainly seems to undermine faith in the evenhanded justice of God—which opens him to the charge of irreligion on the part of his critics. But the fact remains that if even a few instances of lifelong "success" can be pointed out for ungodly men, ideal justice is not always demonstrable for God's providential dealings in this life. Stern judgment in the life to come is the only possible corrective for this apparent triumph of wickedness. Post-mortem retribution is clearly taught in both Testaments—compare Psalm 9:17; Isaiah 5:14-15; 30:33; Ezekiel 32:22-25; Matthew 7:13; II Thessalonians 1:8-9—although more clearly in later times than in the age of Job. But what Hebrews 12:5-8 discloses about God's attitude toward those whom He does not discipline with misfortune is that such forbearance on His part only serves to remove all hindrance from their sliding into eternal hell.

2. (21:17-21) The wicked may or may not be stricken with the calamity that God intends for them, but retribution will befall his children. Yet how does this serve to punish the ungodly sinner himself, if he never sees this affliction with his own eyes in this life? When he is dead and gone, what does it matter to him?

3. (21:22-26) In His inscrutable judgment God allots to one man good health and prosperity to his dying day; to another He apportions a life of bitter deprivation. Yet they both end up in the same pit, where their corpses are consumed by maggots.

4. (21:27-34) Zophar should honestly face the fact, testified to by travelers from foreign lands as well, that there are indeed cases of wicked men who have become wealthy and influential, and have been buried with honor by their survivors and friends. In the face of these exceptions it is absurd and grossly misleading to follow the simplistic rationale that he is preaching.

IV. The Debate Concluded: The Third Cycle (22-31)

A. Eliphaz Denounces Job's Criticism of God's Justice (22)

1. (22:1-11) "Realize, Job, that man's goodness does not add to the happiness of God; therefore it cannot be for His own advantage that God would send prosperity to some men and calamity upon others. Hence the cause of success and disaster must lie within those who receive them from the hand of God" (vv. 1-3).

a. (:4-5) Therefore Job is absurd in claiming that it is for his own godliness that he has been punished by the Lord. Job must have committed many sins that occasioned his affliction.

b. (:6-11) Job must have withheld pawned clothing from his penniless relatives, denied water to the thirsty and food to the starving, and victimized widows and orphans for such severe judgments to have befallen him from the Lord. Only such cruelties as those could account for the flood of misfortune that has overwhelmed him.

At this point the circular reasoning that characterizes the three critics comes out in its most blatant form. Even though Job has always maintained the highest reputation for uprightness and generosity in his entire community, in a society where no secrets could possibly be kept from the general public in regard to inter-personal relations, Eliphaz conjures up out of his dogmatic theory a whole list of offenses and crimes that have somehow been kept secret until now. This paragraph exposes the bankruptcy of his theology in dealing with tragedies such as Job's.

c. (:12-20) No matter how remote God may seem to be from the earthly level of mankind, Job must not for a minute imagine that He cannot see all of the evil committed by wicked men. For all those who have attempted to hide their misdeeds from the Lord or to do things to suit themselves, as if He could do nothing to punish them, have later found to their sorrow that the God whose bounty they had flouted knows how to bring a flood of destruction upon them and sweep them away. (The implication here is that Job has been craftily concealing his sins from his fellow men, vainly hoping that God would not find out about them either.) And when that happens, the righteous people (like Eliphaz and his friends) have occasion to rejoice in God's righteous enforcement of justice upon those who have trampled upon the moral law.

d. (:21-30) Eliphaz now makes another altar call, eloquently urging Job to confess his sins and seek the Lord's forgiveness. He has only to put away his sin and he will receive not only forgive-ness but also the joy of restored fellowship with the Almighty, who always stands ready to forgive the contrite in heart. "Best of all, your new life of godliness will make you a real influence for good in restoring others who have likewise fallen into sin." Thus Eliphaz shows that he is basically concerned for Job's welfare, despite all the harsh words that have been exchanged between them. But Eliphaz firmly insists that Job must give up pretending that he is a victim of undeserved misfortune. He will simply have to confess his secret sins and abase himself in the dust of abject contrition!

B. *Job Responds to Eliphaz That God Knows*
   He Is Without Guilt, and Yet in His Providence
   He Permits Temporary Success for the Wicked (23–24)

1. (23:1–7) Job again turns away from his critics and expresses his yearning to plead his cause before Him, and hear from His lips the reasons for his cruel misfortunes. Then at last the case would be satisfactorily settled and the mystery of God's unaccountable disfavor would at last be cleared up.

2. (23:8–12) "Up until now I cannot find Him anywhere, no matter what direction I go. Yet I feel sure He is testing me through all my afflictions in order that He might refine me like pure gold (a classic affirmation of the second answer to the problem of undeserved suffering—see pages 20–21). All my life until now I have kept very close to the Lord in my daily walk, and have treasured His Word more than any food for my body." No higher standard than this could be set for a New Testament believer! And yet Job lived before any of the Bible was written. Nevertheless he knew what God was telling him and cherished the faith handed down to him from Shem and Noah, even though it had not yet been committed to written form.

3. (23:13–17) "And yet even if I could appear before Him to plead my case, how could I stand before the awesome sovereign of the whole universe, who decrees and performs whatever He pleases? I feel terrified at the thought of a personal confrontation, and yet I feel I must confront Him somehow, despite the thick darkness that hides Him from my view."

4. (24:1–12) Job deplores the slowness with which God deals with the wicked in this life, even though in the end (and in the life to come) they meet with cursing and oblivion. But if only the Lord would appoint days for hearing and deciding cases, as human judges do! How gladly Job would then apply to the omniscient judge of all the earth for the adjudication of his cause!

a. (:2–12) All kinds of wrongdoing and oppression go on, with the stealing of land and of livestock, the victimizing of widows and orphans, the reducing of the poor to the status of wandering beggars, starving and half-naked. Children are seized from their penniless mothers in order to pay for their debts. Indigent day laborers are paid hardly enough to keep body and soul together, even though they work hard at processing the olive harvest and the vintage. All of this misery goes on in the city without any intervention from God, who leaves the oppressors undisturbed and unpunished.

Modern critics who assign a late date to the composition of Job interpret passages like these as reflecting the harsh oppression of Judah during the Babylonian exile in the sixth century B.C. But in this context it is quite obvious that Job is talking about the victimizing of the poor and disadvantaged classes of his society by the unscrupulous upper classes, who disregard all sanctions for the protection of the helpless in their own community. There is no hint of foreign invasion or conquest in this complaint; it only denounces the kind of hardhearted injustice that has always been practiced in civilized society ever since towns and cities were first organized.

b. (:13–17) Added to social injustice there is the problem of outright crime: the robber who murders his victims after dark, the adulterer who defiles other men's wives by night, the burglar who under the cover of darkness breaks into the homes of those who are sleeping. They seem to get away with their wickedness for a time, without hindrance from God.

c. (:18–25) And yet the curse of God catches up with the ungodly, and they are snatched away to the grave without leaving

any lasting achievements behind them, their lives a tragic waste
and their names wiped away by ignominy. Their transient security
turns out to be elusive, their pride is finally humbled to the dust,
and they join their erstwhile victims in a common grave. "Who of
you can gainsay me in this?" Job asks.

C. *Bildad Scoffs at Job's Direct Appeal to God (25)*

1. (25:1–3) God is transcendent above all of His creatures, for
He controls all of the stars above and the forces of nature on
earth (including, of course, the moral order).

2. (25:4–6) How then can a mortal creature maintain that he is in
the right as he contests the dealings of the Almighty? If not even
the heavenly bodies are exempt from His judgments, how can a
mere worm like mortal man have the slightest hope of prevailing
against God in a court of justice?

Here Bildad seems to be misinterpreting Job's position on
seeking out a fair hearing before God. Job is not trying to win out
over God; he simply wants to find out how God feels about him
(in view of his unparalleled disasters), considering that the Lord is
quite aware of Job's innocence.

D. *Job's Rejoinder to Bildad: God Is Indeed Perfectly Wise and Absolutely Sovereign in Punishment of the Wicked, But Not in the Stereotyped, Simplistic Way Described by My Critics (26–27)*

1. (26:1–4) With biting sarcasm Job reacts to Bildad's brief
outburst by rating him as a complete failure as a counselor to the
bereaved. Instead of encouragement to the depressed or understanding insight for the dejected he has offered only unfeeling
bombast, denunciation devoid of God's spirit of compassion!

2. (26:5–11) "How different from your petty-minded harshness is the God for whom you claim to speak—before whom Sheol (Hades) and all its inhabitants (the souls of the dead) lie in anguish, exposed to His awesome gaze! For He is the almighty creator of the starry heavens, who set the earth in the midst of empty space ("He suspends the earth over nothing"), and stored the waters of heaven in clouds that do not burst with their weight, as they cover over the light of the moon."

Many Bible students have commented on the remarkable agreement of these statements by Job with the discoveries of modern astronomy and meteorology—beyond the understanding of any of Israel's neighbors in the ancient Near East. The suspension of planet Earth in empty space was a concept hardly known to ancient science. Especially significant is the knowledge of the circular shape of our sphere implied in verse 10: "He has inscribed a circle" (the verb here is *ḥūg*—"make a circle, go in a circle"), a prescribed boundary (*ḥōq*)—"on the surface of the waters." This suggests the horizon between sky and sea, which demonstrates the curvature of the earth's surface as well as its circularity.

3. (26:11–14) Before Him the mighty powers of nature tremble with awe: the very foundations ("pillars") of the heavens shake at His thunder, the surging sea ("Rahab") that once covered the whole surface of earth He restrained within bounds (Gen. 1:7). The reference to "the fleeing serpent"—*nāḥāsh bāriᵃḥ*—indicates either the titanic forces of natural catastrophe or possibly a constellation in the sky. But even staggering manifestations are but a slight indication of the full scope of God's power.

4. (27:1–6) Job strongly reaffirms his own honesty and integrity before God and also the character of God (in contrast to his three critics, who have tried to defend God's perfect justice by dishonest argument). He therefore refuses to admit that their doctrine of the punishment of every sufferer conforms to the truth of God's providence or to the realities of human experience. To his dying day he will not admit to crimes that he never committed, no matter how bitterly they accuse him.

5. (27:7–12) Far from impugning God's administration of the moral law—as Job's critics accuse him of doing—Job firmly insists that godless men are not heard by the Lord in their times of distress (since those are the only times they call upon Him at all). He is glad to extol God's mighty power and His ways of dealing with evildoers, and so to instruct his muddleheaded "comforters," with their all-too-limited understanding of divine providence.

6. (27:13–23) The fact of the matter is, says Job, that ruthless worldlings who achieve so-called success bequeath a curse as a heritage for their children, no matter how numerous they may be. They will be slain by the sword or the plague, or the money they inherit will soon disappear and end up in possession of the law-abiding, and the mansions bequeathed to them will crumble to ruins. The wealth of the wicked may be suddenly snatched away from him, and he will be overwhelmed by a flood or hurricane of disasters.

In contrast to his scathing critique in chapter 21, where Job was decrying the fallacy of his critics' simplistic formula of sure retribution in this life in the case of all sinners, here he opens up a wider horizon for the scope of God's penal dealings with evildoers. Here in chapter 27 he asserts that all unrepentant sinners, no matter how rich or influential they may become, will either meet with crushing disaster in this life or their posterity will waste away in misery. This does not mean that guilt may be validly inferred from the misfortune a man may experience—the position maintained by Job's adversaries—but it does mean that unconverted evildoers will sooner or later, in this world or the next, be overtaken by the righteous judgment of God, and that their descendants will be saddled with the baleful consequences of their wickedness.

E. *The Search for Transient Treasures Contrasted*
   with the Discovery of True Wisdom,
   Which Transcends All Other Treasures (28)

1. (28:1–11) Proceeding from the matter of retribution, Job now turns to the question of the highest goals for which man should strive. Precious metals, and baser metals as well, are to be found in mines, those long, dark galleries that men dig out to reach their silver and gold, their iron and bronze.

a. (:3–4) To obtain these ores the miners willingly risk their lives in the pits and shafts they have dug. As the miners chip away at the rock for gemstones and gold in tunnels that even the wild beasts and birds would never descry, they encounter underground springs in their search for hidden treasure.

b. (:12–19) But search where these men will, the far greater treasure of true wisdom eludes them. It cannot be dug for or uncovered in the depth of the sea; no market can sell it to them, even for the price of precious metals or gemstones such as sapphires, crystal, jasper, or topaz—jewels that seem like ultimate value to most of mankind. Note that a lack of wisdom soon leads to a loss of wealth, even in the practical affairs of this life.

c. (:20–28) No earthly creature knows where wisdom or understanding are to be found—not even Abaddon or Death (*māwet*) with all of their superhuman knowledge can do more than report a rumor about this true wisdom (*ḥokhmāh*). The only one who really knows what it is and where it is to be found is the Lord God Himself (v. 23).

God knows because He sees the entire universe and has established both the winds and the waves, the lightning and the rain of the mighty thunderstorm (vv. 23–26).

God has revealed what true wisdom consists of, namely, the fear of the Lord (Yahweh): *yir'at 'ᵃdonāy,* that godly reverence for the Lord and His revealed will that controls the motivation and attitudes of God's children. To a person who has this fear of the Lord in his heart, what matters most is the will of God and His glory.

This fear of the Lord, if genuine, leads inevitably to hatred and avoidance of evil (*sûr mēra'*). There is no true godliness that is not characterized by a hatred and an avoidance of sin.

F. *Job's Concluding Complaint*
and Solemn Disclaimer of Iniquity (29–31)

1. (29) Job longingly recalls his former high standing in society.

a. (:1–6) Job remembers the days when God cared for him and blessed his home with His holy fellowship, and even granted abundance to his many children.

b. (:7–17) In public everyone used to show Job appreciation and respect—even the princes and nobles. As a judge in the court Job protected the rights of widows and orphans. As a wealthy bene-factor he helped the poor and the orphan, comforted the dying and the widows, and showed both justice and loving-kindness toward the disadvantaged as against their oppressors.

c. (:18–20) "Back in those days I felt completely secure and confident as to my future, living in good health and vigor."

d. (:21–25) Job continues, "Back in those days people listened to my opinions and judgments with the greatest appreciation and respect; they treated me as a top-ranking authority, to whom they looked for leadership and comfort in time of need."

2. (30) To this noble past Job contrasts his miserable present, in which everyone mocks and despises him in his degradation.

a. (:1–8) But as things are now, even the children of wandering desert riffraff—whom Job would not have deigned to employ with his sheep dogs, and whom all society banished and despised—"it is their children who now mock me and heap abuse upon me."

b. (:9–15) "Not only do these street urchins detest me but they even plot my destruction like a besieging army and threaten my very life."

c. (:16–19) "But even apart from them, the agony of my disease threatens to strangle me and cast me into the dust on which I sit."

d. (:20–23) "I pray to the Lord in vain, for even He turns upon me with ruthless power and smashes me about as if He meant to send me off to Sheol beyond the grave."

e. (:24–31) "Even though I always helped others when they were in trouble, I now receive from both God and man nothing but unfeeling neglect and indifference, no matter how loudly I lament or how sorely my body is racked with fever and pain."

Here Job sinks into a quagmire of self-pity and discouragement, largely because of a strong feeling that God no longer really cares about him—for reasons he cannot begin to fathom. We should perhaps observe at this point that after a long and unremitting bout with physical illness, augmented by the badgering he received from his judgmental human critics, it is no wonder that he fell into such a mood of depression. Even for New Testament Christians who know of all God's "exceeding great and precious promises" and understand that tribulation no more demonstrates God's rejection of us than it did of His own Son on Good Friday, it might prove difficult to maintain peace and poise when we have to face a similar combination of bodily pain and human abuse.

3. (31) Job takes a solemn oath as to his innocence of wrongdoing.

Note that the legal basis of this curse-invoking oath is to be found in the impasse resulting from a series of serious charges leveled at him by his three critics, who have absolutely no evidence to support their claims except for a mere inference derived from their own theological dogma.

a. (:1-4) In his preamble to the oath, Job fully recognizes the law of just retribution for sin, whether in thought or in overt deed: "Is it not ruin for the wicked, disaster for those who do wrong?" (v. 3, NIV). To illustrate the sanction against evil desire— even though not carried out—Job points to the commonest type of temptation for a male observer of female beauty: the emotional impact made by the sight of an especially charming and attractive young woman.

Fully aware of the allure of this baited trap, Job has solemnly committed himself to use his eyes as a faithful steward of God's grace: he will never allow his admiration of such beauty to seduce his heart into personal desire. Here Job shows a clear understanding of the tenth commandment, with its sanction against coveting the wife of one's neighbor. Yet there is no verbal resemblance whatever between Job 31:1 and Exodus 20:17—a circumstance strongly pointing to the fact that the author of Job had no knowledge of the Mosaic Decalogue. This is significant evidence for a date of composition earlier than the time of Moses; it is difficult to explain how even a Solomonic date of authorship could be reconciled with this apparent ignorance of the wording of the Ten Commandments—especially if the book was composed originally by a Hebrew author!

b. (:5-8) Job next disclaims any dishonesty in business relationships. He has never misrepresented facts in order to overreach others in commerce of any kind. He has never cheated in the weighing out of goods for sale or money for purchase. (Prior to the introduction of coinage in the seventh century B.C. all payments in silver had to be weighed in the scales.) Nor has he ever coveted other men's possessions or tried to deprive others of their property in an unfair or illegal manner. In confirmation of this avowal of blamelessness he invokes a divine curse upon his crops and upon his continuing possession of property if he has not told the truth in this regard.

c. (:9-12) Job now turns his attention to the sin of adultery, or guilty relations with another man's wife, in contradistinction to

the involvement with a young, unmarried woman referred to in
verses 1-4. He solemnly avers that he has never fallen into such a
heinous and shameful sin as that, and he prays that if he ever has,
his own wife may be dishonored as he has dishonored another's.

d. (:13-15) Next Job deals with relations to his employees and
slaves, whom he regards as entrusted to him by God as fellow
heirs of the grace of God (v. 15: "Did not He who made me in the
womb make them?" NIV)—a most enlightened insight for a man
of his time! He affirms that he has always treated them justly and
fairly and with due consideration, as one who shall have to give
an accounting for them before God. Observe the implied teaching
that all men at the end of their earthly life will have to give an
accounting before God for all their deeds "done in the body."

e. (:16-23) Job now deals with some of the reckless accusations
that Eliphaz had hurled against him in 22:6-9—offenses against
the poor and needy. He invokes the curse of bodily dissolution
upon himself if he has refused the pleas of the poor, left widows
helpless against their foreclosing creditors, refused to give food to
fatherless children or to take them into his own home when they
were destitute, or failed to give clothing to the naked or assistance
to orphans without sponsors in a court of law. Because of his fear
of displeasing the God of grace or of tarnishing His divine glory
through ungodly behavior, Job has always been scrupulous in
befriending the disadvantaged members of his society.

f. (:24-34) This next stanza covers various sins of meanness,
selfishness, and dishonesty: gloating over the misfortune of an
adversary (to say nothing of invoking a curse upon him), a nig-
gardly withholding of hospitality at his dining table or of lodging
to the visiting stranger, or of keeping his own misdeeds concealed
for fear of public condemnation. If he has ever been guilty of any
of these offenses, he only wishes that his accusers might step
forward and present their firsthand witness against him.

g. (:35–37) Having pled not guilty to all of these transgressions and wrongs, covering a whole gamut of personal and social offenses familiar to his society, Job declares his eagerness to receive any written accusations (complete with specifications and particulars) that his detractors might choose to bring against him. For then at last he would be in a position to take them up and refute them one by one. Such a prosecutor he would welcome like a prince, for this man would at least be open and above-board, rather than operating by baseless inference and insinuation as his three critics have been doing.

h. (:38–40) Job's last asseveration pertains to his stewardship of all his real estate and of his tenants who rent quarters from him. He has never withheld wages from his hired men or unfairly imposed upon his renters. And if he is not telling the truth about this, he prays that his grain fields may become overgrown with briars and weeds as a token of God's curse upon them and upon their earthly owner.

With this all-inclusive and comprehensive oath Job closes his case before his three accusers, and he never is quoted as speaking to them again during the last eleven chapters of the book. So far as mortal men are concerned, Job's words are finally concluded. Nor do his critics have any more to say to him.

V. The Speeches of Elihu (32–37)

A. Elihu Enters into the Debate to Break the Impasse (32)

1. (32:1–5) This is a prose introduction for Elihu, son of Barachel, a younger man who has listened in on the discussion until it finally bogged down in a stalemate. His insights prove to be valuable as a critique of both sides of the controversy and as a theological preparation for the speeches of Yahweh in chapters 38–41. In one sense Elihu serves as an arbiter between Job and his

critics, for he rebukes the three counselors in regard to their
unsupported accusations and consequent inability to silence Job.
On the other hand he severely castigates Job for his belligerent
self-justification and his unfair criticism of God. But his most
important role is that of an advocate for the wise and loving
providence of God. In some ways he can be considered as the
most acute theologian of them all, and he throws more light upon
the central problem of undeserved suffering than any other
speaker in the book (except for God Himself, of course, in the
prologue and epilogue). He is displeased with Job for the way he
attempted to justify himself and prove himself in the right, at the
expense of God's righteousness and integrity. He shows that Job
has overlooked the possibility that suffering may be permitted by
the Lord for wise and benevolent purposes, and that the only
proper response of a true servant of God is a posture of humble
acceptance and uncomplaining submission. What Job needs to
realize is that even though he may be innocent of any and all of
the charges the three critics have leveled against him, his resentful
attitude toward God manifests an insubordination bordering on
arrogance. It is for this sinful presumption that he needs to
humble himself in abject repentance. Significantly enough, even
though Job makes no verbal response to Elihu whatever, he finally
complies with that counsel and roundly condemns himself as a
presumptuous fool, casting himself completely upon God's mercy
(40:3-5; 42:3). Elihu thus serves as a key figure in this whole
drama, and despite his occasional unfairness in his criticism of Job,
he succeeds as a counselor, where Eliphaz, Bildad, and Zophar fail
abysmally.

2. (32:6-9) Elihu injects himself into the discussion with becoming modesty, explaining that he had held back until that point,
feeling that the older and more experienced thinkers should
express their viewpoint before a younger man like himself should
venture to reason with them on the important issue at stake. Yet
he ventures to suggest that younger people also may receive

understanding and insight from the Spirit of God, who is the source of all true wisdom.

3. (32:10-14) "But now," says Elihu, "since I have first listened to you four experts and given careful attention to all of your discussion, it is time for me to add my opinion, especially since the three of you have not come up with a real solution to the problem presented by Job's calamities. With all of your vigorous argumentation you still have failed to prove Job to be wrong in his claim to be guiltless of any secret and unconfessed transgressions to account for his disasters. Therefore I am going to follow a totally different approach, for I have not involved myself in argumentation with him at all."

4. (32:15-22) "Now that the other three have talked themselves out and have nothing more to say, it is time for me to express what I have upon my heart, for I feel a tremendous burden to share it with you" (v. 19, "Inside I am like bottled-up wine, like new wineskins ready to burst!" NIV).

"And please understand that as I speak I will not argue as a partisan of either side in this controversy; I will express myself honestly and forthrightly, without any attempt to curry favor from either side."

B. *Elihu Charges Job with Presumption in Criticizing God,*
   Not Recognizing That God May Have a Loving Purpose
   Even in Allowing Job to Suffer (33)

1. (33:1-7) "Now, Job, I want you to give me a fair hearing as a sincere friend who may be guided by the Spirit of God in what I tell you. You do not need to feel at all defensive toward me, for I am only a fellow human being and make no pretension of being a specially anointed prophet from God."

2. (33:8-11) "You have charged God with treating you unfairly and unjustly, even though you have been guilty of no wrong, and you have accused Him of persecuting you in a malicious way as if He regarded you as His enemy" (cf. 13:27).

3. (33:12–22) "Job, you have drawn false conclusions from your unhappy circumstances, and have charged God with not answering your prayers."

a. (:14–18) "One way in which God answers is through significant dreams of warning, by which He intends to deter us from a contemplated sin or to deliver us from the snare of pride."

b. (:19–22) "Another way the Lord speaks to us is through severe and protracted illness, with considerable loss of weight and of appetite, bringing to us a prospect of dying in bed."

4. (33:23–28) "In such a case, if some angel (*mal'āk;* "messenger") intervenes on his behalf as a mediator (*mēlîṣ;* "interpreter"), first he may teach the patient what he needs to learn from his painful and frightening experience, and then he may intercede for him before the Lord, urging that he has found a ransom (*kōper;* "an atonement") for him that he might not die."

Note how closely the role of this interceding angel resembles the role of the risen Christ, who according to Hebrews 7:25 "always lives to make intercession for them," that is, for those who come to God through Him. Elihu seems to speak with prophetic inspiration as he describes this angel of mercy.

a. (:25) As the Lord grants that prayer of intercession, the ailing believer is restored to complete health and vigor once more.

b. (:26–28) But, more important than physical recovery, the healed man establishes a closer personal relationship with God than ever before, and rejoices in Him with a new joy over His wonderful forgiveness and grace. Then he becomes an active and enthusiastic witness for the Lord and gladly confesses his sin and praises God for His marvelous grace, by way of earnest testimony before others. Thus the Lord knows how to bring "the peaceable fruit of righteousness" (Heb. 12:11, KJV) out of a bitter experience of affliction.

5. (33:29–30) In His faithful, persevering grace God may send such experiences of illness and suffering into a person's life in order to save him from hell and restore him to the light of a living fellowship with God.

6. (33:31–33) "If I have said anything so far that is unfair to you or inappropriate to your case, please tell me now. Otherwise let me continue and try to convey the wisdom the Lord has taught me in this matter."

At this point Job has no comment to make, possibly because he can find no fault with what Elihu has brought up thus far. Therefore Elihu feels free to continue.

C. *Elihu Declares That Job Has Impugned God's Integrity*
   in Upholding the Moral Law, and Has Claimed
   That It Does Not Pay to Lead a Godly Life
   in This Ungodly World (34)

1. (34:1–9) "By all means we must honestly face the basic issue Job has raised, that we may come out to sound conclusions."

a. (:5–6) Job has contended that he is completely innocent and free from blame, and yet God has unjustly denied his rights and made him look like a liar. He claims that the Lord has unfairly afflicted him with incurable illness.

b. (:7–9) "But such an accusation against God makes Job sound like a skeptic who undermines the faith of others by his cynicism. Like ungodly worldlings, Job puts himself on the side of scoffers who deride the scruples and lifestyle of the godly and claim that it is futile to try to please God."

This stern denunciation does not represent Job's true position at all, but Elihu is arguing here that Job's earlier accusations against God lead logically and inevitably to a complete rejection of religious faith. In one sense this charge of irreligion is grossly unfair, in view of the fact that Job has exalted the Lord as the wise and holy sovereign over the universe in terms even more eloquent than those of any of his collocutors (see chaps. 27–28). But he has also been guilty of emphasizing the apparent success of evildoers throughout their career in such a way as to give aid and comfort to godless materialists (see 21:7–21). To be sure, Job later tried to balance this pessimism as to the triumph of "poetic justice" in this life by a more careful and devout statement concerning the ultimate enforcement of God's justice upon the unrepentant sinner (whether in the misery of his descendants or in the retribution he has to face in the life beyond [see 27:8–23]), but even this has not eliminated the cynical impression left by his earlier outburst against Zophar. So far as Job's overall assumption is concerned—that he is competent to find fault with God's administration of justice, or with the constancy of His love—Job is grievously in error to imagine for even a moment that he who is a mere creature, deriving from his creator any comprehension of righteousness or love that he may possess, could possibly rise above the source from which he received them. This grossest of fallacies—into which any of us may fall whenever we ask of God the rebellious question, "Why me?"—must be exposed for its folly and be completely rejected!

c. (:10–15) Elihu lays down a basic principle for every thinking man ("you men of understanding") to consider: that God as the origin and essence of all good can never do what is evil or commit wrong. As judge of the universe His commitment to the moral law will always impel Him to mete out just punishment upon the wicked (v. 12, "It is unthinkable that God would do wrong, that the Almighty would pervert justice!", NIV). There is no greater force than His and no higher authority than He; who or what, then, could possibly make Him deviate from absolute justice?

Indeed, as the moment-by-moment sustainer of all His material creation, He would only have to withdraw His life-giving Spirit and all creatures would immediately perish.

d. (:16-20) Elihu now drives home the implications of God's complete sovereignty and absolute righteousness: the Lord is completely beyond our competence to criticize or find fault with in regard to His enforcement of justice. Even the kings, the nobles, the princes, and all the wealthy of this earth are judged by Him without favoritism or partiality, and may suddenly be cut off by death in the middle of the night. Even the mightiest of men are subject to speedy judgment and sudden removal from the earth.

e. (:21-30) No evil or evildoer can successfully hide from His all-seeing gaze, or deceive the Lord with false evidence, in the way that human judges can be deceived.

(1) (:24-25) Since He has full knowledge of the wickedness of unworthy rulers, He suddenly removes them from their dishonored thrones and replaces them with others (cf. Ps. 2:9; Isa. 11:4).

(2) (:26-28) The objects of His condemnation had been those who turned from the will and law of God and ruled their people to suit themselves. But the victims of their tyranny were heard by God and He plunged their oppressors into sudden destruction.

(3) (:29-30) Therefore even in cases where He does not respond with speedy vengeance, but sees fit to withhold His retribution until such time as He deems best, we may rest assured that He will maintain His righteous control over the affairs of nations and men, and never allow injustice to enjoy a lasting triumph. Such is the testimony of all human history, ever since the great deluge. The forces of wickedness and falsehood have always—sooner or later—met with destruction and passed away.

f. (:31-33) In dealing with this heavenly judge a mortal man should come not with a demand to God that He justify His providential ways but rather with a prayer that the Lord may forgive the petitioner for whatever he may have done amiss. And if he has committed wrong unwittingly, he should pray that God may teach him what it was—with the sincere resolve never again to commit that offense. This, then, is the normal and established way for a believer to approach his Lord. But if perchance Job knows how to obtain God's attention and favor without any willingness to repent, this is an approach that Elihu knows nothing about, and of which he would need to be informed. (Note the gentle irony imbedded in these three verses.)

g. (:34–37) Job should realize that his language toward God (as he reproaches Him for unfairness and lovelessness) has created an impression among thoughtful listeners that he has spoken without spiritual insight, and that he therefore needs to be sorely chastened for such impious speech and for rebellion and scoffing.

Here again Elihu seems guilty of misconstruing the intent of Job's remarks and making him out to be in a state of rebellion toward God and of scorn at the faith others have expressed in regard to the Lord's integrity in administering judgment. To ignore so completely the many affirmations that Job has expressed concerning the wisdom and holiness and ultimate justice of God is decidedly unfair and uncalled-for. Elihu would have done better to attempt to bring all that Job had said about God into some sort of unified focus, rather than to highlight the negative and ignore the positive. It is interesting to observe that Job does not even bother to defend and explain further his own true position, and thus to protest against Elihu's misrepresentation of his stance toward God. Perhaps he was too tired of argumentation to rise to the challenge that Elihu presented to him.

D. Elihu Urges Job to Wait Patiently for the Lord to Act
   Whenever and However He Sees Fit (35)

1. (35:1–8) Job should understand that it is futile for him to suppose that God is ever going to vindicate him as innocent of any evil sufficient to warrant all of his misfortunes, while at the same time he has argued that it does not pay to lead a godly life. In the face of such provocative cynicism how could God possibly clear him?

a. (:4–8) We must remember that since God is infinitely transcendent, our moral or immoral conduct on earth does not directly affect Him, whether to injure Him or to benefit Him. Our moral behavior affects only our fellow human beings.

b. (:9–11) Men who are suffering under oppression are willing enough to turn to God with prayers for relief and deliverance. But who ever lifts his heart to God in grateful praise for His goodness in bestowing an intelligence upon man that distinguishes him from brute creation, and for His kindness in putting songs of joy in the hearts of His children, even during the lonely hours of the night?

c. (:12–16) Yet God cannot be expected to answer prayer for the wicked and the proud; indeed He will give them no heed. Therefore He can hardly be impressed by a person like Job, when he on the one hand claims that he has in faith laid his case before Him and that he will patiently wait for His disposal of it and on the other hand suggests that God is not much concerned about wickedness and injustice (judging by the way He leaves evildoers undisturbed). These two positions tend to cancel each other out, and for all of his eloquent words Job does not make any sense.

But here again I must point out that Job has never claimed that God does not ultimately bring the wicked and proud into condemnation; he simply pointed out that in some cases, at least, no visible retribution overtakes the wrongdoer until he dies (see 21:13), even though his children will indeed perish by the sword and all his wealth will fall into the hands of others as his memory becomes shrouded with infamy. It may well be that Job needs to repent for some of the things he once or twice affirmed in a way discreditable to God's justice and derogatory to His faithful love.

But he never asserted that God is truly indifferent about the moral behavior of man, as Elihu has mistakenly inferred.

E. *Notwithstanding Job's Criticisms, the Lord Almighty*
   Still Remains the Avenger of Injured Justice,
   Even Though He May Administer His Providence
   in Ways Beyond Our Comprehension (36)

1. (36:1-4) Elihu is ready to contend that God is a perfectly righteous judge, despite any contrary appearance; and Elihu knows what he is talking about (rather than merely mouthing traditional opinions), for he has been taught this truth directly by God Himself.

2. (36:5-15) God faithfully rewards the righteous and lovingly disciplines the wayward through suffering.

a. (:5-7) Infinite and transcendent though He is, God has a personal concern for mankind, meting out death to the unrepentant wicked, avenging the wrongs of the oppressed, and exalting the godly and sincere to kingly status (whether in this life—like Joseph ben Jacob—or in the life to come).

b. (:8-12) By allowing the wayward to fall into the chains of affliction the Lord brings them to repentance for their rebellion and pride, that they may return to obedience and serve Him under His blessing. But if they then refuse to repent and will give Him no heed, they perish by the sword in their folly.

c. (:13-15) The ungodly will not cry for God's mercy or help even when He chastens them by affliction. Such will have to die young, as hardened and incorrigible degenerates like the homosexual cult-prostitutes at the heathen shrines. Nevertheless God uses even their sorrows to speak to them about judgment and grace.

3. (36:16–21) So also in your case, Job, God means to incite you to escape from the painful straits into which you have fallen (like some sinner who has gone astray), and you must realize that that redemptive love of His is worth far more than any wealth or temporal profit (*kōper* means "ransom, recompense," in verse 18, rather than NIV's "bribe") that might turn you aside from goals that matter for eternity. (Verse 17 seems to refer to Job's preoccupation with seeing all the wicked immediately judged and punished by God, rather than his waiting for Him to follow His own methods and timetable.)

a. (:20–21) "Beware of the embitterment in your own soul when you center your thoughts on the dark night of death overtaking the wicked; and beware of speaking presumptuously against God ("turning to evil"), which you seem to choose in preference to the patient endurance of your affliction."

Elihu seems to feel that Job has not been deriving from his trials that spiritual deepening and sweetening that the patient endurance of his afflictions was intended by God to bestow upon him.

4. (36:22–33) Elihu reminds Job that in His sublime perfection God is not subject to criticism or performance ratings by man; all of His management of the forces of nature and the races of men are far beyond our correction or improvement.

a. (:22–26) No mortal creature is in a position to reprove the Lord for any of His providences, or to instruct the God who is his own instructor. All we can do is marvel at Him.

b. (:27–33) Just as wonderful as His management of the precipitation cycle and the loud, crashing thunderstorms is His use of rain and storm to fructify the fields and furnish mankind with their food—and the cattle as well, with their pasturage.

F. *Elihu Continues to Argue, from Man's Inability
to Understand Fully God's Workings in Nature,
That Human Observers Can Hardly Expect
to Understand Adequately His Dealings
in Administering Justice and Mercy (37)*

1. (37:1–13) As if hearing the approach of a great thunderstorm, Elihu depicts the terror instilled by the terrible lightning flashes and the deafening thunder that follows it—the mighty voice of the Creator addressing His puny creatures. Nor can they understand how God sends down from heaven the snow and the cloudburst of rain, causing both man and beast to scurry for shelter and suspend all their activities while the storm rages on. Or else He sends the freezing ice and snow, and even the lakes become hard as stone. Thus God may send His storm clouds to wreak destruction, or else to bless the thirsty earth with water as a loving benefit to man.

2. (37:14–18) "Job should carefully consider the implications of the perfect wisdom that God displays in managing the weather; how can mortals like us draw up a case to make Him alter His decree? No more than we can gaze directly at the sun in the sky! Look now," says Elihu, "the Almighty approaches us from the north in His splendor and majesty, incomparably greater than we in His power, His righteousness, and His justice, which He administers in kindness and mercy rather than to oppress His creatures. Let everyone therefore revere Him, for He will take notice of all those who are wise in heart!"

At this point Elihu can speak no further, for the wind and the storm have burst upon them all, and only the voice of God can be heard. But Elihu has already made his contribution to a proper understanding of what has happened to Job, and the possible factors that are involved in his various disasters. He has shown Job that God may send misfortune upon the innocent for benevolent purposes: to humble his pride, to intensify his sensitivity toward sin, to heighten his feelings of gratitude to the Lord for

His faithful love, and above all—in Job's case—to purge him of all arrogance and self-defensiveness toward God. The right use of suffering leads to a complete and unreserved surrender to the will of God without rebellion or willfulness of any kind. The extensive references to the awesome power of the wind and lightning and storm appropriately pave the way for the speeches of Yahweh Himself, as He breaks down all that remains of Job's rebelliousness and complaint against the providential dealings of the Lord, and prepares him for complete restoration and a new life of peace and joy and fellowship with God.

VI. Jehovah's Addresses to Job (38–41)

A. No Man Is Competent to Pass Judgment
   upon the Dealings of the Almighty (38:1–38)

1. (38:1–11) Now at last Job's wish—a personal audience with God—is fulfilled. This means the Lord has not abandoned him after all, and cares enough about him to rebuke him face to face. At last the lines of communication have been restored once again, much to Job's relief—even though the communication is largely one of reproach.

God's opening words are full of rebuke and challenge to His beleaguered servant. "Who is this that darkens counsel [NIV's translation, "my counsel," finds no support in the Hebrew text] by words without knowledge?" (The term *'ēṣāh* means here "good counsel, wise counsel"—which Job forsook insofar as he fell into bitter reproach against God and combative defense of himself against the insinuations and attacks of his three critics.) Job has neither seen the issues clearly, so far as his misfortunes are concerned, nor shed light upon them for the benefit of others. Through his false inference of God's alienation from him because of the disasters He allowed to befall him, he only contributed confusion and darkness. Despite his occasional insights of faith and his eulogies concerning God's wisdom, perfection, and power, the overall trend of his argumentation is in the direction of mystifying paradox and puzzlement. He would not even try to answer the reasoning of Elihu as he sought to bring Job to a better understanding of the blessings to be found through suffering—even undeserved suffering.

Yet Yahweh summons Job to rouse himself to consider what He is about to say to him, and be prepared to answer him like a thoughtful, intelligent adult ("Brace yourself like a man"—*geber*, i.e., a strong, capable, responsible man). God is saying, long in advance of Isaiah 1:18, "Come, let us reason together" (as litigants facing each other in a court of law).

(:4-11) God now puts a challenging series of questions to Job concerning his competence to pass judgment upon the operations of divine providence: "Were you present at the creation of planet Earth, when its dimensions were marked out by the master designer?" "Did you at that time observe the setting up of the forces (of solar gravity, circumsolar revolution with its centrifugal force) that established its position and orbit within the solar system—like the footings and cornerstone for a building?" "Or were you there when the angels sang their chorus of admiration and praise, along with the stars of heaven that observed the fashioning of the earth?" "Were you watching when the Lord confined the waters of earth to oceans, seas, and lakes, rather than permitting them to cover the great land masses as they did before, and when the suspension of earth's moisture in the form of huge clouds allowed the dry land to appear, protected against the lashing assault of the breakers upon the shore?"

The emphasis upon the confinement of destructive or chaotic forces suggests the perfect balance and control of all the rest of God's creation, including His moral universe.

2. (38:12-15) The competence to criticize or correct the Lord in dealing with matters of justice presupposes at least a lower level of experience in controlling the rotation of earth (in the sequence of night and day), and administering its government in such a way that all the wicked might be shaken out of it or be broken in their power, even as the terrain of earth is shaped by the great geologic forces set in motion by God Himself. "Have you had that experience, Job, to equip you to improve upon My ways of governing the destinies of mankind?"

3. (38:16-30) God puts similar questions to Job concerning his knowledge of the oceans and continents, the sources of light and darkness, the physical laws of snow and lightning and rain and ice. Such an understanding of the great processes of nature should form an elementary basis for the far more difficult and involved operations connected with issues of punishment, reward, discipline, and justice in the management of human affairs. (It would be difficult to find anywhere else in world literature any more beautifully poetic description of the processes of wind and weather than that which is set forth in this chapter of Job.)

4. (38:31-38) The range of interrogation now shifts to astronomy and meteorology. To be qualified as a critic of God Job ought to have developed some expertise in managing the great constellations such as Orion and the Bear. Or at least he ought to demonstrate competence in directing thunderstorms, winds, and rain—to say nothing of implanting reason and intelligence in the mind of human observers affected by this weather, and regulating the weather to save the earth from sunbaked drought.

B. *God Probes Job's Knowledge in Controling*
   and Feeding Wild Animals and Birds (38:39—39:30)

1. (38:39-41) Has Job learned how to care for the needs of the lion or the raven as they seek nourishment?

2. (39:1-4) Or does Job know how to provide for the mountain goats or the wild deer as they give birth to their young, and as their offspring learn to care for themselves without the aid of human tutors or nurses?

3. (39:5-12) Or what about the wild and untamable donkey that shuns all human habitation to roam the wastelands? Or the giant aurochs that no man can capture or tame for the plow or the threshing floor? The implication is that the domesticating of these intractable beasts would be much easier than the proper administration of justice and grace in human affairs.

4. (39:13-18) And then there is the uncatchable ostrich, rather foolish in leaving her eggs unprotected and careless of her young, and yet so swift that no horseman can overtake her.

5. (39:19-25) Or again, there is the war-horse, that, while trained to be sure by its owner, nevertheless despises the noisy menaces of an opposing battle line and enjoys charging into its midst regardless of war cry or trumpet blast. ("If you cannot cope with his fearless assault, Job, how can you expect to improve upon God in meting out judgment upon sin?")

6. (39:26-30) Look at the soaring hawks or the eagles that build their nests beyond the reach of man, and from the clifftops swoop down upon their prey with unerring skill and capture it for their young. (God knows how to equip them and provide for their needs. Can you?)

C. *The God Who Made the Behemoth and the Leviathan*
Is Far Beyond the Competence of Man to Criticize
or Correct (40-41)

1. (40:1-8) At God's rebuke for accusing Him of injustice, Job responds with abject confession of his own unworthiness and his inability to speak any more in his own defense.

But a surrender of self-defense is not quite enough to clear Job of his arrogance in charging God with lovelessness and unfairness as he tries to exonerate himself of all blame. Therefore the Lord summons him—now that he has at last obtained his often-expressed wish to stand before God and argue his case—to face up to his guilt in questioning God's justice in order to justify himself.

2. (40:9–14) "If you think to contend with Me about the way I deal with men in the light of their innocence or guilt, then you must demonstrate an ability on your own part of unleashing your judicial wrath at all the proud and compelling them to abase themselves before the bar of justice. Then you must crush them completely and consign them to the grave as retribution for their sin. Only when you have accomplished all of this will I concede your ability to justify your criticism of Me."

It is interesting to observe how unsparing the Lord is in His reproof of Job—almost as severe as Elihu had been. If Job is ever to become reconciled to Yahweh after his long and agonizing period of alienation, then he must face his own offenses of pride and self-defensiveness. To be sure, these two traits emerged only in connection with a genuine concern for honesty, and a firm resolve to avoid settling for any false solution to the mystery of his unparalleled combination of misfortunes. The three counselors did their best to brainwash Job into an acceptance of the lie that it was his own hidden crimes that had brought on his disaster. Job was unshakably loyal to the truth when he rejected that explanation as culpably simplistic and offensive even to God Himself. But in the pressure of unremitting pain and humiliation Job was guilty of accusing the Lord of unfairness and lovelessness for allowing him to fall into such distress and disgrace when he had apparently done nothing to bring it on. Yet in this misjudging of the Lord on the basis of adverse appearances Job had fallen into the same grave fallacy into which his three critics had fallen, when they too had misjudged Job on the basis of mere appearances. In other words, Job's criticism of God was almost as unfair and as uncalled-for as the three friends' criticism of Job.

3. (40:15–24) Consider the mighty, unconquerable *behēmōth* (an amplificative plural from *behēmāh*—a larger quadruped, whether domesticated or wild). This huge and invincible river creature was almost certainly a hippopotamus (it was known to lie hidden among the lotuses and reeds of the Jordan River in ancient times, though now it is confined to Africa), which was "first among the works of God." That is, he was the largest and heaviest of the animals known to residents of the ancient Near East. There may have been an especially gigantic variety that flourished in the Jordan in those days, and as such he may have outclassed even the elephant, which after all could be captured by man through traps and could even be mortally wounded by attacking from the rear and severing its tail at the stump by a deft stroke of the saber. But neither technique would subdue the hippopotamus. He simply could loll in the river and feed on the vegetation that floated down from the hills, and never be threatened by the floods that might come, since he could neither be drowned nor swept away. The hippopotamus, then, is cited as a creature of God too fierce and formidable for man to subdue. (It should be added, however, that hippos of more normal size were often captured in the Upper Nile and imported to Roman arenas for the entertainment of the public. They may even have been maintained in zoos, just as in modern times.)

4. (41) Yahweh next adduces another example of a fierce and untamable beast, namely, Leviathan, a name derived from the root *lāwah* or *lāway,* meaning "twist, wind." Since Leviathan leaves a churning wake in the waters (vv. 30–31), has a mouth "ringed about with . . . fearsome teeth" (v. 14, NIV), is protected with rows of impenetrable shields (vv. 15–18), and sneezes out spray like sparks of fire in the glint of the sun, it is probably to be identified as a gigantic crocodile. Since it is spoken of as too strong and dangerous to capture, it could hardly be an import from the Nile (i.e., an Egyptian crocodile). It is a creature close enough at hand for Job and his compatriots to observe firsthand or even to attack as big game (v. 8). And since he is described right after Behemoth (which is clearly a denizen of the Jordan), it is most likely a monster that likewise inhabited those waters.

a. (:1-11) This fierce and intractable reptile is completely beyond
the power of man either to capture or to tame, for his body is
impervious to harpoons or spears, and his frightful appearance as
he lunges forward against any would-be attackers throws them
all into demoralization and panic.

The Lord uses the example of this overwhelmingly terrible
brute that He has created in order to bring out the inference that
the God who fashioned Leviathan is infinitely more irresistible in
His power, and is not to be confronted or defied by mortal man.
(NIV renders *hiqdīm* as "stand against"; NASB makes it "Who has
first given to Me, that I should repay him?"—which is less suitable
to this context.)

b. (:12-34) This crocodile, Leviathan, is invincible because he is
protected by impenetrable armor that cannot be removed by any
hunter and also by a mouth full of sharp, jagged teeth, dealing out
death to anyone he bites. His back is covered with rows of tightly
fitted shields, impenetrable by sword or spear. His very appearance
fills the would-be attacker with utter dismay, for as he sneezes
out the river water from his nostrils, it looks like sparks of fire,
and the vapor from his nostrils wreathes his head like smoke.
Even the powerful muscles of his neck are impossible for a hunter
to bend back, and the scales that cover his chest are as hard as
rock. It is no wonder that even mighty men (*'ēlîm*) are dismayed
and fall back when he comes charging at them (v. 25), for their
finest weapons of iron and bronze cannot pierce him, and neither
arrows nor slingstones nor clubs make the slightest impression
upon him (vv. 25-29). Even his underside is protected by jagged
scales like sharp potsherds, and his mighty tail makes the water
foam with its thrashing (vv. 30-32). In short, Leviathan is unconquerable before all his foes and fiercer than the proudest of his
adversaries.

The inference here again is that the God who so constructed
and equipped Leviathan is incomparably greater, and completely
beyond the power of man to hold Him to accountability before
their human tribunals or philosophical judgments. Both Behemoth

and Leviathan, therefore, are living demonstrations of the over-whelming power of God that surpasses all human capacity to rebuke or check—an infinite superiority that extends also to His administration of the moral law in His providential dealings with men. Job must therefore completely surrender to the perfection of God's wisdom, righteousness, and power, even though he may not understand the reasons that led God to permit all of the calamities that came upon him. Job must therefore face the fact that even though he could not understand why God has so dealt with him, nevertheless he must not presume to criticize the Lord as unfair, unkind, or unfaithful to him. He must maintain com-plete trust in Him even as he passes through the dark valley of heartbreak and suffering, and hold firmly to the conviction that God Almighty does all things well, and that He never, never makes a mistake—and that He never ceases to love and care about His own!

VII. The Epilogue:
Job's Repentance and Vindication (42)

A. Job Passes Contrite and Unsparing Judgment upon Himself (42:1-6)

1. (42:1-2) Overwhelmed by all of these demonstrations of God's infinite wisdom and power, Job confesses his sinful folly in attempting to limit or define how God must exercise His sover-eignty. He gives over all of his former resistance and reproach as he acknowledges, "I know that Thou canst do all things, and that no purpose of Thine can be thwarted" (v. 2).

2. (42:3) Next, Job unreservedly condemns himself for raising objections against what God had decreed. He quotes God's own challenge to him in 38:2 ("Who is this that obscures My counsel without knowledge?"), and then admits with a broken heart,

"Surely I spoke of things I did not understand, things too wonderful for me to know" (NIV).

The essence of Job's error was drawing conclusions on the basis of mere appearances. Even though he freely acknowledged God's right to remove from him all the gifts that He had once bestowed upon him—all his wealth and even his ten children (1:21; 2:10)—and realized that the furnace of affliction may produce the purest of gold (23:10), yet Job had challenged God in three areas: the worthwhileness of allowing a baby to live who would in later life become the victim of such affliction as Job's (3:11-23; 10:18); the kindness or fairness of God in making Job the target of His arrows (6:4; 7:20), persecuting him unceasingly with nightmares and spasms of pain (7:14-19), and multiplying his wounds without cause (9:17); the justice of God in making him appear guilty even though he was actually innocent (9:20-23), and in actually mocking the righteous in their affliction (9:23).

To be sure, as Job says himself, he spoke without knowledge, for had he known that God had highly honored him by choosing him to be a test case in refutation of Satan, he would not have been tormented by the question *"Why?"* and he would have patiently borne his trials like a hero in an arena.

3. (42:4-5) Job is overwhelmed by the privilege of being directly and audibly addressed by God Himself, even though the conversation turned out to be a rebuke for him rather than a forensic vindication. Even though he as defendant can find no answer to give to the Lord by way of his own defense (a right he had longed to claim, in 23:3), yet he has received more than enough compensation for all his woes in that he has been directly addressed by the Lord, with opportunity to respond to Him personally, and with the thrilling privilege of beholding the manifestation of the Lord before his very eyes.

4. (42:6) The last feature of Job's response is an unqualified condemnation of himself as utterly unworthy of the Lord's grace. He who had been so stoutly defending himself and clearing

himself of guilt before men is now in the presence of God overwhelmed by the guilt of having criticized and misjudged the Lord.
"Therefore," says Job, "I despise myself and repent in dust and
ashes" (NIV). He has at last entered into the peace of absolute
surrender to his Redeemer. There is no more controversy, no
more resentment, no more rebellious questioning. It is enough
for Job that the Lord really cares about him; He has cared enough
to devote four chapters of loving rebuke to His bewildered and
bitter servant. The pall of silence and alienation has lifted, and Job
may speak to his God once more, in the confidence that God loves
him and is always ready to hear his voice. And for a true man of
God, that is what matters the most!

B. God's Condemnation of Eliphaz, Bildad, and Zophar
   (42:7–9)

Having dealt with Job and having brought him to total submission through heartfelt and sincere repentance, Yahweh now turns
His attention to the three critics who had so unjustly and cruelly
badgered Job in his misfortune.

1. (42:7–8) Much to the astonishment of these three self-
assured theologians, who had ostensibly taken up the cudgels in
defense of God and orthodox doctrine concerning His sure, swift,
and unerring justice, they suddenly find themselves defendants
before the court of God, and hear from His lips condemnation for
their bad theology and false teaching. "You have not spoken of
Me what is right as My servant Job has" (v. 7).

a. (:7a) What was it that was wrong in these critics' teaching
about God? By this time in the discussion it should be clear that
their watertight dogma about the unfailing relationship between
sin and retribution was framed to exclude the possibility of God's
using affliction in order to purify and strengthen the faith of
truly obedient believers. This prerogative of employing affliction
in order to purge faith and promote the growth of spirituality in

the servant of God—with added effectiveness in his counseling and assisting others who are experiencing deep grief—was completely excluded by the theology of Eliphaz and his associates. Furthermore, such a rigid system led them to the extremes of mental cruelty that they meted out to an innocent victim like Job. For any teacher to pretend to speak for God and to teach without love, but with a desire to believe evil of another person without any supporting evidence whatever, is to malign and grievously misrepresent the Lord whom he professes to serve. Their narrow construction of the meaning of suffering as only and always retribution for sin would have led them to conclude from the sufferings of Jesus of Nazareth that He too must have been guilty of gross and terrible sin. From this standpoint it is easy to see why Yahweh was so indignant with them.

b. (:7b) But now we must ask what was so very right about what Job had said of God. After all, Job had been sternly rebuked by the Lord during the four preceding chapters, and had been so overwhelmed by his own guilt in unworthily criticizing and complaining against God that he had completely broken down with confession, repentance, and self-condemnation. How could Job then be commended as a true and faithful teacher of the doctrine of God? Two elements are involved here.

(1) Job's repentance was so thoroughgoing and complete that God could cancel out his guilt entirely. Once Job had recognized his folly in judging God's attitude toward him simply on the basis of adverse appearances as altogether wicked and unworthy, it was possible for God to forgive him completely and cleanse him of that sin.

(2) But there remained a magnificent testimony for the Lord in the dogged faith which Job never really surrendered, that God knew the truth about his innocence and that He somehow and in some way would vindicate him. Even though Job bitterly reproached the Lord for his unaccountable plunge from prosperity to disaster, he never renounced Him or cursed Him (as his wife

had urged him to do), nor did he ever question God's wisdom, might, or glory. On the contrary, he set forth the surpassing splendor and perfection of Yahweh in terms far more eloquent than the speeches of the three counselors themselves (who claimed to be God's advocates and defenders).

Furthermore, interspersed between the bitter remonstrances Job voiced on account of his suffering and degradation were heights of insight and faith that spoke of a divine mediator and redeemer, and exalted the Lord as the ultimate vindicator, whom he would be privileged to behold in his resurrection body. This, then, was the essence of the endurance (*hypomenē*) of Job that is held up as a model for Christians in James 5:11.

These elements, then, are summed up by the Lord in this seventh verse as that which is right (*nᵉkōnāh*).

c. *(42:8-9)* The Lord directs the three counselors to seek forgiveness through blood sacrifice. But they will not be accepted by the Lord unless they are represented by an acceptable mediator. And to their chagrin the mediator whom God specifies is none other than Job himself—that disreputable culprit whom they had so contemptuously vilified and condemned. Nothing could have been so humiliating, so utterly disconcerting, as to be compelled to supplicate that forsaken reject of society, who had so impudently discarded their counsel and refused all of their calls to confession and repentance. Anybody but Job! Nevertheless, if they were to avoid the wrath and punishment of the Lord Almighty, they had no choice but to go crawling to Job and admit that they were completely wrong about him, and had condemned him unjustly.

It is significant, by the way, that Elihu was not included in God's judgment of condemnation. He was not required to offer any atonement offering, presumbly because despite his occasional harshness and misinterpretation of Job's complaints, he had put his finger on Job's true sin—pride and insubordination toward God. In that sense he had prepared Job for humble submission to

Jehovah's admonition and rebuke in His speeches from the whirlwind.

But the three critics obeyed the Lord in this transaction. They not only besought Job's pardon but also his kind intercession on their behalf, as they brought him their animals to sacrifice to the Lord on their behalf as their burnt offering. Job apparently felt no hesitation in complying with their request, especially since he knew it was the will of God for him to serve as their priest in this matter.

C. Job's Restoration to the Favor of His Community and Relatives (42:10–11)

1. (42:10) Job had to be willing to set aside all feelings of resentment toward his three persecutors before he could receive the fullness of God's blessing. "After Job had prayed for his friends, the LORD made him prosperous again" (NIV). An unforgiving servant of God can never enjoy real peace of soul or true fellowship with his Lord as long as he withholds complete forgiveness from those who have wronged Him. Any lingering ill will corrodes like acid in the soul and makes pure joy in the Lord an utter impossibility.

2. (42:11) Now at last Job's brothers and sisters and all his former friends, who had shunned him and neglected him entirely as a pariah, rallied around him with comfort and encouragement. Doubtless they had heard that Yahweh had pronounced in his favor and had miraculously healed him of his painful boils. Not only did they express their sympathy and concern, but they also contributed a piece of silver and a ring of gold, each one of them, as a tangible expression of their love and support. (The word rendered as "piece of silver" is *qᵉsīṭāh*, a specific weight of silver bullion probably in excess of a shekel; it is also mentioned in Genesis 37:28 in connection with the sale of young Joseph as a slave to the Midianite merchants traveling down to Egypt. The

"ring of gold" is *nezem,* which is known to have been used of a nose
ring, as in Genesis 24:22, where it is specified as weighing half a
shekel.)

D. *Job's Renewed Prosperity and Lengthened Span of Life*
   (42:12–17)

1. (42:12) Job apparently made excellent use of this relief fund
by purchasing new livestock, which bred even more prolifically
than those that the raiders had taken from him. He eventually
built up his herds to 14,000 sheep, or twice the number he had
lost. The same was true of his camels, oxen, and donkeys; they all
doubled in number, and he became twice as wealthy as he had
ever been before. Why did God bless him in such an amazing
fashion? Probably because the Lord wanted all of Job's generation
to know that he had come through his ordeal in such a way as to
honor and glorify God, and to set an example of how future
generations of believers should behave as they went through
testings and trials. The only way in which Job's contemporaries
could be certain of God's vindication of Job was by His restoring to
him all that he had lost, two times over. It was a case which
warranted special favor, because this man had disproved the
cynical contention of Satan that all men are moved by self-interest
as they practice religion. Job exemplified a believer who loved God
for His own sake, entirely apart from His blessings.

2. (42:13) Moreover the Lord assuaged the heartbreak of the
loss of all ten of Job's children by granting him seven new sons
and three lovely daughters. Interestingly enough, the daughters
were more of a sensation than the sons were. At least they won
top honors for their beauty, and their names are given (the sons'
are not). Their names are quite distinctive, although only one of
them has survived in modern times, namely, Jemimah of pancake
fame! But apparently even Keren-happuch ("Horn of eye shadow")
married, and presented her proud father with grandchildren. Who

could have mothered all these children? Presumably not Job's first wife, who must have been worn out after bearing her husband the first ten children. Nor is it likely that she and Job ever reconciled after her renunciation of the Lord in 2:9, and Job's rebuke of her as a "foolish woman." We may safely assume that Job obtained a new and younger wife, with whom he enjoyed a happy and peaceful life.

The final verses, 16–17, record Job's living on for another 140 years after his restoration, and his joy at seeing his family line continue on until his great-grandchildren were growing up. "And so he died, old [at least two hundred years old!] and full of years" (NIV).

And I might add that even after his long and eventful life drew to its close, his memory did not die with him, but lives on to this day, nearly 3,000 years later—as the hero of the oldest written book in the Holy Bible.

VIII. Concluding Remarks

A careful reading of the Book of Job results in a profoundly moving experience. No more overwhelming combination of misfortunes could be imagined than those that came upon this sincere and godly servant of the Lord. No more shocking disparity could be found between what was deserved and what was meted out to this hero of the faith. At the beginning of written revelation came this solemn warning that the just are to live by faith, not by sight. They are to understand that repentance for sin and commitment to their divine Lord and Savior will not necessarily lead to a life exempt from heartbreak, frustration, and pain. The "slings and arrows of outrageous fortune" (to borrow a phrase from *Hamlet*) may be part of God's plan for even the most sincere and most spiritually minded believer. Those who follow the Lord Jesus may have to walk with Him through rejection, slander, frustration, and disappointment, even as He did during His earthly ministry.

The experience of walking through the valley of the shadow may well be their portion even as it was David's, and that of his messianic descendant, Jesus of Nazareth.

The life story of Job is given to us in order that we may understand very clearly that it is "through much tribulation that we enter the Kingdom of God," as Paul reminded the new converts at Lystra, where he nearly had been stoned to death. Into the lives of nearly all of the outstanding servants of the Lord, both in the Old Testament period and in the days of the New Testament apostles, came persecution, bereavement, and heartbreaking loss. They enjoyed great triumphs and success, as Hebrews 11 reminds us, for "through faith they subdued kingdoms, wrought righteousness, obtained promises, stopped the mouths of lions [as Daniel did], quenched the violence of fire [like Shadrach, Meshach, and Abednego], escaped the edge of the sword, out of weakness were made strong, waxed valiant in fight, turned to flight the armies of the aliens." Conversely, "others were tortured, not accepting deliverance, that they might obtain a better resurrection. And others had trial of mockings and scourgings, yea, moreover of bonds and imprisonment. They were stoned, they were sawn asunder [like Isaiah], they were tempted, they were slain with the sword. They wandered about in sheepskins and goatskins, being destitute, afflicted, tormented . . . they wandered in deserts and in mountains, and in dens and caves of the earth." The apostolic author of these stirring words drew upon the experiences of all the heroes of faith, from the time of Abel to the leaders of the Maccabean wars of independence, in order to remind the Christians of his own time (some of whom had already been cruelly martyred by Nero, and were destined for persecution and death in the days of Vespasian, Titus, and Domitian) that the life of true faith has always included tribulation as well as triumph, and suffering as well as success. And yet it is precisely through these heartbreaking discouragements that God brings about our greatest good and His greatest glory. As Paul wrote in Romans 8:37, "Nay, in all these things we are more than conquerors through him that loved us" (KJV). The vantage point here is, of course, not the earthly perspective but the heavenly. It involves the glorious certainty that born-again believers have a Christ-guaranteed mansion in glory (John 14:2), and in contrast to the brief span of threescore years and ten referred to in Psalm 90:10, we shall be there with our Redeemer throughout all eternity. Or at least we shall be with Him wherever He is, even during His thousand-year reign upon earth (Rev. 1:6; 20:4) and throughout the ages to come (Rev. 22:5).

Let no scoffer reply that he has little use for the promises of "pie in the sky by and by," for these are much better than the alternative of punishment "with everlasting destruction from the presence of the Lord and from the glory of His power" (II Thess. 1:9). According to the Word of God—the only book on earth that records the certainties of God rather than the conjectures of men—these are the only possible destinies awaiting the souls of the dead, after their opportunity for salvation here on earth has finally run out.

It is therefore possible to understand and correctly evaluate the sufferings of the innocent Job—a man whom God Himself regarded as "blameless" and "upright"—only from the perspective of eternity. The real purpose of life is not to attain personal ambitions or desires, but to glorify God. Job himself questioned, at first at least, whether a life was worth living if it was to be marked by deep sorrow and crushing misfortune at its latter end (Job 3:20–26). But as he wrestled with depression and grief and the tormenting accusations of his false friends, even Job came to see that "when he has tested me, I will come forth as gold" (23:10, NIV). "I know that my Redeemer lives, and that in the end he will stand upon the earth. And after my skin has been destroyed, yet in my flesh I will see God" (19:25–26, NIV). In other words, however bad things get down here, it will all be worth it when we get up there. As Paul put it so beautifully: "For which cause we faint not; but though our outward man perish, yet the inward man is renewed day by day. For our light affliction, which is but for a moment, worketh for us a far more exceeding and eternal weight of glory; While we look not at the things which are seen,

but at the things which are not seen: . . . but . . . are eternal"
(II Cor. 4:16–18, KJV). This was the insight from a true and sterling
servant of the Lord who had already by that time been flogged
and imprisoned and nearly stoned to death for the cause of the
gospel. Three times he had suffered shipwreck, and faced peril
from robbers, from Christ-rejecting Jews and Gentiles, and from
all sorts of dangers in the city and in the wilderness and upon the
face of the deep. This superb model of godly living and consecra-
tion had found himself "in weariness and painfulness, in watch-
ings often, in hunger and thirst, in fastings often, in cold and
nakedness" (II Cor. 11:27, KJV)—to say nothing of the intense
emotional and spiritual drain of pastoral care and agonizing inter-
cessory prayer for his converts in the many cities where he had
labored for the Lord (see II Cor. 11:23–28). The apostle Peter
admonishes us: "Beloved, think it not strange concerning the fiery
trial which is to try you, as though some strange thing happened
unto you; But rejoice, inasmuch as ye are partakers of Christ's
sufferings; that, when his glory shall be revealed, ye may be glad
also with exceeding joy" (I Peter 4:12–13, KJV).

The united testimony of Holy Scripture is that we are not to be
shocked or surprised when misfortune strikes us or touches our
dear ones. Those testings that come our way are allowed or
appointed by God in His sovereign wisdom and unfathomable
love in order to bring out the finest and best spiritual development
we can possibly achieve. Worldly prosperity and success contribute
but little to our spiritual growth. But a godly response to suffering
and disaster brings us closer to the Lord and makes us more
completely dependent upon Him. If Job had continued in the
prosperous and happy condition described in chapter 1, his life
would never have counted for the Lord in the way that it did. God
chose him for the honor of demonstrating before Satan and all
the unbelieving world that true faith is not simply an enlightened
form of self-interest (as the skeptics claim), but that it involves a
sincere love of God for His own sake, even apart from all His
temporal blessings. It is important for us to see that in a very
profound sense the patriarch Job is a model for us as well. There

is a sense in which we too, whenever we are overtaken with
sorrow or pain, bereavement or loss of health, or whatever the
affliction may be, are privileged to demonstrate a genuine love for
God for His own sake, and entirely apart from those earthly
blessings that the children of this world feel they must have in
order to be happy. We are to confirm by our attitude and behavior
under stress that the Lord Jesus is primary in our life, and that we
are willing to trust His love and His sufficiency all through the
dark night of pain. Like Paul we must be able to testify to our
conviction "that neither death, nor life, nor angels, nor princi-
palities, nor powers, nor things present, nor things to come, Nor
height, nor depth, nor any other created thing, shall be able to
separate us from the love of God, which is in Christ Jesus our
Lord" (Rom. 8:38, KJV).

To all true believers, whether to ourselves or to others, this
sublime rationale for undeserved suffering brings a glorious relief.
It delivers us from doubting the love of God or misunderstanding
His will. It keeps us from becoming mired down in the fallacious
assumption that misfortune proves that we have not been "living
right"—the damnable error of Eliphaz, Bildad, and Zophar. "If we
suffer with Him, we shall also reign with Him" is the promise in
II Timothy 2:12. This does not refer only to those persecutions
from men who are opposed to the gospel and hate the cause of
Christ, but also to any affliction or sorrow that comes into our
life as a member in the body of Christ. As we by faith commit the
painful experience to Him, He becomes a part of it in His love and
concern for us. In that sense, then, we endure our suffering *with
Him*. And as we deal with that suffering in such a way as to reflect
His divine nature, and thus to glorify His holy name, we shall
throughout the everlasting future share in His eternal splendor
as well.

This, then, is God's answer to the problem of undeserved suffering. Even through the bitterest misfortunes of life God works
all things together for good to those who love Him, to those who
are called according to His sovereign grace to be His own (Rom.
8:28). This is *the* answer to the problem, and it is the *only* answer

that really makes any sense. All other answers fall woefully short, and they ultimately lead to unrelieved bitterness and despair. But the solid conviction that God's love in Christ extends to His suffering children despite all of their agonizing trials, and that He has a wise and worthy purpose through it all, is enough to carry them triumphantly through the deepest waters or the fiercest trials with their banner of love and of faith still high above them.

From what I have just said, it is clear that God has an answer to the problem of undeserved suffering. But what is not so clear is the proper manner of imparting this answer to the afflicted, especially as they are passing through the earlier and more intense forms of grief. From the poor example of Eliphaz, Bildad, and Zophar we can learn about what we should *not* do. Let us survey briefly the mistakes that led them to fail in their mission of mercy.

The three counselors at first tried to show appropriate sympathy (they were willing to wait in silence for a week as they watched Job and felt for him in his deep grief), but they failed to achieve empathy. That is to say, they made no effort to see Job's afflictions from his viewpoint; they were content to analyze them from afar. They never asked themselves, "How would I feel if *I* had lost all my children at once, and if *I* had been violently robbed of all my wealth, and all my trusted servants had been murdered, and if *I* had fallen victim to a painful and loathesome disease—and my own wife had left me in disgust?" Instead, they studied his case from the standpoint of general theory, seeking out a likely cause for this calamitous effect.

The counselors also attempted to argue with Job about theological issues and preach at him in a condemnatory way, rather than encouraging him to pour forth all of his feelings. A victim of misfortune needs to be convinced that the prospective counselor really cares about him and is doing his best to understand him. Of this loving, personal concern there is hardly a trace in the comments of any of the three.

These men assumed that they knew the reason for Job's misfortunes, as if they had direct communication with God and had been explicitly informed that Job had committed some grievous sin (or series of sins) that he had somehow successfully kept hidden from public knowledge. But this assumption was built upon a simplistic theory that since all sin is punished with disaster, therefore all disaster must result from a sin that deserved it. "Consider now: Who, being innocent, has ever perished?" asked Eliphaz (4:7, NIV). The answer to that is very obvious: Many have perished, being innocent. One has only to think (to borrow an example from later times) of the massacre of all the male babies in Bethlehem who were two years old or younger. But to Eliphaz it is heresy to suppose that misfortune could ever befall one who has not deserved it. Job's protest that some experience calamity who never deserve it and some escape disaster who richly deserve it on account of their ungodliness is sternly rejected as tending to "undermine piety and hinder devotion to God" (15:4, NIV). But a Christian counselor must never assume that every victim of misfortune has done something very wicked to bring it on. There are always a few cases—Joseph and David, Isaiah and Jeremiah, Judas Maccabeus, Stephen the martyr, James the son of Zebedee, the apostle Paul, and indeed the Lord Jesus Himself, for whom this adverse judgment would be totally wrong.

It was egregiously offensive and insulting for the three critics to conclude without any corroborative evidence that Job was guilty and needed to repent. And yet this assumption was necessarily implied by each of them as they addressed their eloquent altar calls to Job with fulsome assurances of God's forgiving grace. Even so it is essential for counselors in our own day to avoid drawing any adverse conclusions concerning their counselees, unless they are very sure of the facts on the basis of outside evidence, or else (preferably) on the basis of admissions made by the victim himself. In general it is far better to draw the advisee out by way of sympathetic enquiry, to see if something in his past might have led to his misfortune, rather to try pushing or badgering him into making self-damaging admissions. This latter approach will certainly establish the counselor as an enemy rather than a friend, so far as the unhappy victim is concerned. At times like this he needs a lifeline rather than a whip.

It was a sign of complete incompetence for the three visitors to respond to Job's lamentations with angry denunciation. Any indication of anger or rejection on the part of a counselor means that he is unsuited to his task, and he will be a hindrance to comfort and recovery rather than a help. A true comforter must be gentle and kindly in his approach to his counselee; otherwise he is virtually useless. A person in Job's plight needs sympthetic understanding rather than denunciatory criticism.

An effective advisor should be very slow to condemn a victim of misfortune for expressing deep grief and bitter complaint. Grief is an almost unavoidable consequence of bereavement, maltreatment, or pain. Those who lose loved ones achieve quicker and healthier recovery if they allow themselves, and are allowed by others, to express their grief. Characteristically that grief will go through a regular series of phases, which should be sympathetically expected and understood. It is reassuring to tell the mourner that his behavior is normal and typical for most people who are in his plight. If he can simply understand his current phase as part of a common pattern of recovery, he is granted some hope that in due time he too may make a satisfactory recovery. Thus, instead of sternly denouncing Job for his mournful complaint that he should never have been born, or that at least he should have died at birth, Eliphaz should have told him in a kindly way, "I know how you feel, my friend, and I can understand how at a time like this you might question whether your life is worth while any longer. It is only natural to long for release from what seems like an absolutely intolerable situation. But I wonder, is it not possible that the God whom you have loved so long and served so well is aware of your present misfortune? I wonder how He feels about all of this?" This approach would have promoted Job's consolation and recovery more effectively than did the frontal assault that Eliphaz and his companions constantly maintained against their helpless friend.

In general it is best for the comforter to establish an empathetic rapport with his counselee as soon as possible, and to give him full opportunity to unburden his heart and express all of the bitterness pent up inside him before attempting to lead him to theological insights into a possible meaning for his experience. Only after that can the scene be set for searching for Scripture-based principles that might help him to understand and to cope with his misfortune. One should be very cautious about quoting the well-known standard Bible verses that apply to times of misfortune and trial. The grieving sufferer is apt to reject these verses as being too trite in their message, and all too easy for a counselor to recite from memory. He may perceive that the counselor has not earned the right, through personal experience, to apply them to the misery of someone else. These verses, and perhaps even those insights that are set forth earlier in this chapter, may lose their helpfulness if they are brought up too soon in the grief process. If there is an underlying anger toward God in the heart of the sufferer, it is more helpful to wait a while before attempting any kind of full-scale Bible instruction. Perhaps it is better to wait until he brings up the matter of Bible teaching on his own initiative.

I can only close this discussion of the message of this sublime book with the prayer that all who study it may feel a bit better prepared than ever before to go through whatever trials the Lord may have in store for them, and to be a better comforter to those who are in any trouble. As the apostle Paul expressed it: "Blessed be the God and Father of our Lord Jesus Christ, the Father of mercies and the God of all comfort; who comforts us in all our affliction so that we may be able to comfort those who are in any affliction with the comfort with which we ourselves are comforted by God" (II Cor. 1:3-4).

Bibliography

For those who wish to do further study I suggest (but do not necessarily endorse) the following works.

Andersen, Francis I. *Job: An Introduction and Commentary.* Tyndale Old Testament Commentary series. Downers Grove, IL: Inter-Varsity, 1976.

Cox, Samuel. *Commentary on the Book of Job.* London: Kegan Paul, 1880.

Davidson, A. B. *The Book of Job.* Cambridge Bible series. New York: Cambridge University Press, 1951.

Delitzsch, Franz. *The Book of Job.* Reprint edition. Grand Rapids: Eerdmans, 1949.

Driver, S. R.; and Gray, G. B. *Critical and Exegetical Commentary on the Book of Job.* International Critical Commentary series. Edinburgh: T. & T. Clark, 1950.

Genung, John F. *The Epic of the Inner Life: The Book of Job.* Boston: Houghton & Mifflin, 1891.

Zoeckler, Otto. *Commentary on Job.* J. P. Lange's Commentary series. Reprint edition. Grand Rapids: Zondervan, n.d.